Fodor's POCKET 2nd edition

istanbul

Excerpted from *Fodor's Turkey*

fodor's travel publications
new york • toronto • london • sydney • auckland
www.fodors.com

contents

maps

Distance Conversion Chart

Kilometers/Miles

To change kilometers (km) to miles (mi), multiply km by .621.
To change mi to km, multiply mi by 1.61.

km to mi	mi to km
1 = .62	1 = 1.6
2 = 1.2	2 = 3.2
3 = 1.9	3 = 4.8
4 = 2.5	4 = 6.4
5 = 3.1	5 = 8.1
6 = 3.7	6 = 9.7
7 = 4.3	7 = 11.3
8 = 5.0	8 = 12.9

Meters/Feet

To change meters (m) to feet (ft), multiply m by 3.28.
To change ft to m, multiply ft by .305.

m to ft	ft to m
1 = 3.3	1 = .30
2 = 6.6	2 = .61
3 = 9.8	3 = .92
4 = 13.1	4 = 1.2
5 = 16.4	5 = 1.5
6 = 19.7	6 = 1.8
7 = 23.0	7 = 2.1
8 = 26.2	8 = 2.4

ON THE ROAD WITH FODOR'S

EVERY TRIP IS A SIGNIFICANT TRIP. Acutely aware of that fact, we've pulled out all stops in preparing *Fodor's Pocket Istanbul*. To guide you in putting together your Istanbul experience, we've created multiday itineraries and quick tours. And to direct you to the places that are truly worth your time and money, we've enlisted a writer who's seen all corners of Istanbul.

British-born **Gareth Jenkins,** who updated all the material in this book, is a writer and journalist who has lived in Istanbul since 1989 and describes his fascination with Turkey as being almost an addiction. He has written three books on Turkish history and culture and is currently researching a fourth.

Don't Forget to Write

Keeping a travel guide fresh and up-to-date is a big job. So we love your feedback—positive and negative—and follow up on all suggestions. Contact the *Pocket Istanbul* editor at editors@fodors.com or c/o Fodor's, 280 Park Avenue, New York, New York 10017. And have a wonderful trip!

Karen Cure

Editorial Director

europe

ICELAND
Reykjavík
NORTHERN IRELAND
SCOTLAND
Edinburgh
Belfast
IRELAND
Dublin
Irish Sea
UNITED KINGDOM
WALES
ENGLAND
Cardiff
London
North Sea
NORW
Bergen
Skagerrak
DENMARK
Hamburg
NETHERLANDS
The Hague
Amsterdam
Rotterdam
GERM
Brussels
BELGIUM
Bonn
Frankfurt
Paris
LUXEMBOURG
English Channel
ATLANTIC OCEAN
0 400 miles
0 600 km
FRANCE
Zürich
Munich
Bern
SWITZERLAND
Lyon
LIECHTENSTEIN
Milan
Ljub
Venice
Monte Carlo
MONACO
Nice
Marseille
Florence
ANDORRA
PORTUGAL
Lisbon
Madrid
Barcelona
Corsica
SPAIN
Sardinia
Balearic Islands
Seville
Granada
Tyrr ienian
Gibraltar
Mediterranean Sea
MOROCCO
ALGERIA
TUNISIA

FINLAND
NORWAY
Gulf of Bothnia
Oslo
SWEDEN
Helsinki
St. Petersburg
Gulf of Finland
Tallinn
Stockholm
ESTONIA
Skagerrak
Kattegat
Göteborg
Riga
LATVIA
Moscow
MARK
Copenhagen
LITHUANIA
Baltic Sea
Kaunas
Vilnius
RUSSIA
RUSSIA
mburg
Kaliningrad
Minsk
rdam
Berlin
POLAND
BELARUS
Warsaw
GERMANY
nn
furt
Kraków
Kiev
Prague
CZECH REPUBLIC
UKRAINE
SLOVAKIA
Munich
Vienna
Bratislava
Salzburg
Budapest
AUSTRIA
MOLDOVA
HUNGARY
Chişinău
CHTENSTEIN
SLOVENIA
Ljubljana
Zagreb
ROMANIA
Venice
CROATIA
Novi Sad
Bucharest
BOSNIA AND HERZEGOVINA
Belgrade
SERBIA
Black Sea
lorence
Adriatic Sea
Sarajevo
YUGOSLAVIA
Priština
BULGARIA
Rome
MONTENEGRO
Sofia
Skopje
Podgorica
ITALY
MACEDONIA
Istanbul
Tiranë
Naples
ALBANIA
Ankara
TURKEY
GREECE
Aegean Sea
Ionian Sea
Sicily
Athens
CYPRUS
MALTA
Crete
Mediterranean Sea

turkey

BULGARIA
Black Sea
Kirklareli
Demirköy
Edírne
Lüleburgaz
GREECE
TEM/E80
Kilyos
Bosphorus
Beykoz
Tekirdag
Istanbul
Iskudar
Keşan
Gallipoli
Dardanelles
Sea of Marmara
Termal
Iznik
Çanakkale
Bursa
Truva (Troy)
Balıkesir
230
Amasra
E10
Zonguldak
Ereğli
Karasu
Safranbolu
Izmit
Düzce
Adapazari
E5
Osmancik
Kızılırmak
Sakarya
Ankara
Eskisehir
Kirikkale
Kütahya
Polatlı
Emir Dagi
Bergama (Pergamum)
Manisa
Gediz
Usak
E96/300
Afyon
Turgutlu
Salihli
Lake Tuz
E90/750
Aksaray
İzmir (Smyrna)
L. Egridir
Ephesus
L. Beysehir
Konya
Söke
Büyük menderes
Denizli
Isparta
Aegean Sea
Ereğli
Bodrum
TAURUS MOUNTAINS
Antalya
Tarsus
Marmaris
Göksu
Mersin
Fethiye
GREECE
400
Alanya
Silifke
400
Anamur
Mediterranean Sea

GEORGIA
ARMENIA
AZERBAIJAN
SYRIA
IRAQ
N
Sinop
Bafra
Boyabat
Samsun
Ünye
Ordu
Giresun
Trabzon
Rize
Artvin
Kars
Ani
Yesilirmak
Çoruh
Suşehri
E390
E80/100
Erzurum
Aras
Ağri
Mt. Ararat
Doğubayazıt
E88/100
Sivas
Kızılırmak
Erçiş
Keban Baraji
Elazig
Muş
Lake Van
Van
Kayseri
Malatya
L. Hazar
Murat
Bitlis
Tatvan
Mt. Nimrod
E99/360
Diyarbakır
Hakkâri
Gölbaşi
Atatürk Barajı
Tigris
Kahramanmaras
Seyhan
Ceyhan
Firat
Şanlıurfa
Mardin
Cizre
Gaziantep
E90/400
Adana
Islâhiya
Iskenderun
Antakya
Euphrates
0
200 miles
0
300 km

istanbul

In This Chapter

Updated by Gareth Jenkins

introducing istanbul

THOUGH IT IS OFTEN REMARKED that Turkey straddles Europe and Asia, it is really Istanbul that does the straddling: The vast bulk of the country resides comfortably on the Asian side. European Istanbul is separated from its Asian suburbs by the Bosporus, the narrow channel that connects the Black Sea, north of the city, to the Sea of Marmara, to the south. (From there it is only a short sail to that superhighway of the ancient world, the Aegean.) The European side of Istanbul is itself divided by a body of water, the Golden Horn, an 8-km-long (5-mi-long) inlet that separates Old Stamboul, also called Old Istanbul, from the "new town," known as Beyoğlu. The Byzantines once stretched an enormous chain across the mouth of the Golden Horn in hopes of protecting their capital city from naval attack. The tactic worked for a time but ultimately failed, after the young Ottoman sultan Mehmet II (ruled 1451–81) had his ships dragged overland from the Bosporus and dropped in behind the chain.

To be sure, more than a mere accident of geography destined Istanbul for greatness. Much of the city's character and fame was created by the sheer force of will of four men. The town of Byzantium was already 1,000 years old when, in AD 326, Emperor Constantine the Great began to enlarge and rebuild it as the new capital of the Roman Empire. On May 11, 330, the city was officially renamed "New Rome," although it soon became better known as Constantinople, the city of Constantine. The new Byzantine empire in the East survived long after the Roman Empire had crumbled in the West.

Under the Byzantine emperor Justinian (ruled 527–565), Constantine's capital flourished. Justinian ordered the construction of the magnificent Hagia Sophia (known as the Aya Sofya in Turkish and referred to throughout this book as such) in 532, on the site of a church originally built for Constantine. This awe-inspiring architectural wonder, which still dominates Istanbul's skyline, spawned untold imitators: Its form is copied by many mosques in the city and elsewhere in Turkey, most notably the Blue Mosque, which sits across Sultanahmet Square like a massive bookend. Under the Byzantines, Constantinople grew to become the largest metropolis the Western world had ever seen. Contemporaries often referred to it simply as the City.

The Ottoman sultan Mehmet II, known as Fatih (the Conqueror), is responsible for the fact that the Hagia Sophia clones are mosques and not churches. It was Mehmet who conquered the long-neglected, nearly ruined Constantinople in 1453, rebuilt it, and made it once again the capital of a great empire. In time it became known as Istanbul (from the Greek *eis tin polin*, meaning "to the city"). In 1468 Mehmet II began building a palace on the picturesque hill at the tip of the city where the Golden Horn meets the Bosporus. Later sultans embellished and extended the building until it grew into the fabulous Topkapı Palace, which can still be seen today.

But most of the finest Ottoman buildings in Istanbul date from the time of Süleyman the Magnificent (ruled 1520–1566), who led the Ottoman Empire to its highest achievements in art and architecture, literature, and law. Süleyman commissioned the brilliant architect Sinan to design buildings that are now recognized as some of the greatest examples of Islamic architecture in the world, including mosques such as the magnificent Süleymaniye, the intimate Sokollu Mehmet Paşa, and the exquisitely tiled Rüstem Paşa.

Istanbul has its modern side, too, with all the concomitant traffic jams, air pollution, overdevelopment, and brash concrete-and-glass hotels creeping up behind its historic old palaces. But the city is more than grime and noise. Paradoxically, its beauty lies in part in the juxtaposition of the ancient and the contemporary. Some of the perks that come with modernity are luxury hotels, designer clothing stores, and Western-style department stores. These are today's monuments, which, alongside the elegant mosques and majestic palaces built by and for yesterday's titans, dominate and define splendid Istanbul.

QUICK TOURS

If you're here for just a short period you need to plan carefully so as to make the most of your time in Istanbul. The following itineraries outline major sights throughout the city, and will help you structure your visit efficiently. Each is intended to take about four hours—a perfect way to fill a free morning or afternoon. How much time you spend at each place will depend on your tastes and priorities, but these brief outlines will give you an idea of which sights and areas make for a logical tour of the city.

TOUR ONE

Make your first stop **Topkapı Sarayı,** the vast palace that was at the heart of the Ottoman Empire for more than 400 years and is Istanbul's number-one tourist attraction. You could easily spend two days here, but at least see **the Treasure Room, the Harem,** and **the Porcelain Collection.**

TOUR TWO

After lunch at one of the restaurants lining Divan Yolu in Alemdar, visit the **Blue Mosque**—so named because it's decorated with 20,000 shimmering blue İznik tiles. Afterwards,

Your checklist for a perfect journey

WAY AHEAD

- Devise a trip budget.
- Write down the five things you want most from this trip. Keep this list handy before and during your trip.
- Make plane or train reservations. Book lodging and rental cars.
- Arrange for pet care.
- Check your passport. Apply for a new one if necessary.
- Photocopy important documents and store in a safe place.

A MONTH BEFORE

- Make restaurant reservations and buy theater and concert tickets. Visit fodors.com for links to local events.
- Familiarize yourself with the local language or lingo.

TWO WEEKS BEFORE

- Replenish your supply of medications.
- Create your itinerary.
- Enjoy a book or movie set in your destination to get you in the mood.
- Develop a packing list. Shop for missing essentials. Repair and launder or dry-clean your clothes.

A WEEK BEFORE

- Stop newspaper deliveries. Pay bills.
- Acquire traveler's checks.
- Stock up on film.
- Label your luggage.
- Finalize your packing list—take less than you think you need.
- Create a toiletries kit filled with travel-size essentials.
- Get lots of sleep. Don't get sick before your trip.

A DAY BEFORE

- Drink plenty of water.
- Check your travel documents.
- Get packing!

DURING YOUR TRIP

- Keep a journal/scrapbook.
- Spend time with locals.
- Take time to explore. Don't plan too much.

head across the street to **Aya Sofya,** the world's largest church until St. Peter's Basilica was built, and **Yerebatan Sarnıcı.**

TOUR THREE

The **Egyptian Bazaar,** also known as the Spice Market, is a worthwhile stop on any tour of this commercially vibrant city. Combine a stroll through this marketplace with a visit to the enormous **Süleymaniye Cami.**

TOUR FOUR

If you can spare a full day, spend it taking a cruise up **the Bosporus.** Even if you only have a few hours, however, a cursory tour via commuter ferry is worthwhile for the incredible views of the city from the water.

In This Chapter

Updated by Gareth Jenkins

here and there

UNTIL THE EARLY 1980S ISTANBUL, with its crumbling ancient buildings, was its own best museum. Most artifacts of the city's past were locked away in storage areas or poorly displayed in dusty, badly lit rooms. But in recent years Istanbul's museums have been transformed. Topkapı Palace, which for 400 years was the palace of the Ottoman sultans, contains a glittering array of jewels, ceramics, miniature paintings, and holy relics. The Archaeological Museum houses one of the most important collections of classical artifacts anywhere in the world. The Museum of Turkish and Islamic Arts holds superb examples of artistry and craftsmanship.

In addition to its fine museums, Istanbul is packed with marketplaces, mosques, palaces, architectural wonders, and a lot of traffic. So, how do you find your bearings in such an unpredictable place? Head for the Galata Bridge, which spans the mouth of the Haliç (Golden Horn). Look to the north, and you will see the new town, modern Beyoğlu, and Taksim Square. From the square, high-rise hotels and smart shops radiate out on all sides. Beyond Taksim lie the fashionable modern shopping districts of Şişli and Nişantaşı.

The residential suburbs of Arnavutköy, Bebek, Yeniköy, Tarabya, and Sarıyer line the European shore of the Bosporus. Look southeast, across the Bosporus, and you can see the Asian suburbs of Kadıköy and Üsküdar. To the south, across the Galata Bridge from the new town, lies the old walled city of Stamboul and Sultanahmet (after the sultan who built the Blue Mosque), with Aya Sofya and Topkapı Palace at its heart. Turn to look up the Golden Horn, and you should be able to make out two more bridges, the Atatürk, favored by cab drivers hoping to avoid the Galata Bridge, and the Fatih, out at the city's northwestern edge.

Numbers in the text correspond to numbers in the margin and on the Exploring Istanbul and Bosporus maps.

OLD STAMBOUL

Old Stamboul isn't large, but it can be overwhelming, for it spans vast epochs of history and contains an incredible concentration of art and architecture. The best way to get around is on foot.

A Good Walk

Begin from **Topkapı Sarayı** ①. Walk back past **Aya Irini,** a smaller-scale version of Aya Sofya. The **Arkeoloji Müzesi** ② is just north of Aya Irini. A small square surrounding a fountain built by Sultan Ahmet III lies just outside the Topkapı Palace gate. Take a right down Soğukçeşme Sokak, a beautiful cobbled street lined with restored wooden Ottoman houses. At the bottom of Soğukçeşme Sokak, just before the entrance to Gülhane Park, take a left up Alemdar Caddesi to **Aya Sofya** ③ and **Yerebatan Sarnıcı** ④. Cross to the far left-hand corner of the small park between Aya Sofya and the **Blue Mosque** ⑤ to Kabasakal Caddesi. Approximately 325 ft along Kabasakal Caddesi is the **Mozaik Müzesi** ⑥, which is believed once to have been the imperial palace of the Byzantine emperors. Backtracking around the southern face of the Blue Mosque, you can see the foundation of the **Hippodrome** ⑦, a Byzantine stadium, stretching northeast for three blocks to Divan Yolu. West of the Hippodrome is **Ibrahim Paşa Sarayı** ⑧; walk to the southwest down Mehmet Paşa Yokuşu to get to **Sokollu Mehmet Paşa Cami** ⑨.

TIMING

Allow approximately 45 minutes to an hour to walk this route, two or more days to take in all its sights. Topkapı Sarayı and the Arkeoloji Müzesi are open daily. The Blue Mosque is also open daily, but the Carpet and Kilim museums within it are closed weekends. Aya Sofya and the Ibrahim Paşa Palace are closed Monday, the Mosaic Museum on Tuesday, and the Kariye Museum on Wednesday. It's best not to visit mosques during midday prayers on Friday.

Sights to See

★ ☺ ❷ **ARKEOLOJI MÜZESI** (Archaeology Museum). A fine collection of Greek and Roman antiquities—including pieces from Ephesus and Troy, along with a magnificent tomb believed by some to have belonged to Alexander the Great—is among the museum's highlights. Since most of the pieces have been removed from the archaeological sites of Turkey's ancient cities, touring the museum can help you visualize what belongs in the empty niches as your tour the country.

Among the museum's sections is one for children, complete with a replica of the Trojan Horse; a special exhibit on Istanbul through the ages; and one on the different settlements at Troy. Because the children's wing is primarily intended for Turkish schoolchildren, the captions there are in Turkish. There are plans to open other special sections, but at press time (fall 2000), these have been hindered by a shortage of staff, which occasionally leads to existing sections being temporarily closed. Outside the museum is a small garden planted with bits of statuary and tombstones. In summer a small café is open.

Admission to the Arkeoloji Müzesi is also good for entry to the nearby **Eski Şark Eserleri Müzesi** (Museum of the Ancient Orient) and **Çinili Köşkü** (Tiled Pavilion). The first museum is something of a disappointment despite its Sumerian, Babylonian, and Hittite

Arkeoloji Müzesi, 2
Aya Sofya, 3
Beyazıt Cami, 11
Blue Mosque, 5
Çırağan Sarayı, 28
Deniz Müzesi, 27
Divan Edebiyatı Müzesi, 22
Dolmabahçe Sarayı, 26
Egyptian Bazaar, 17
Eminönü, 18
Eyüp Camii, 15
Galata Köprüsü, 19
Galata Kulesi, 21
Galatasaray Meydanı, 24
Grand Bazaar, 10
Hippodrome, 7
Ibrahim Paşa Sarayı, 8
Istanbul University, 12
Mozaik Müzesi, 6
Rüstem Paşa Cami, 16
Sokollu Mehmet Paşa Cami, 9

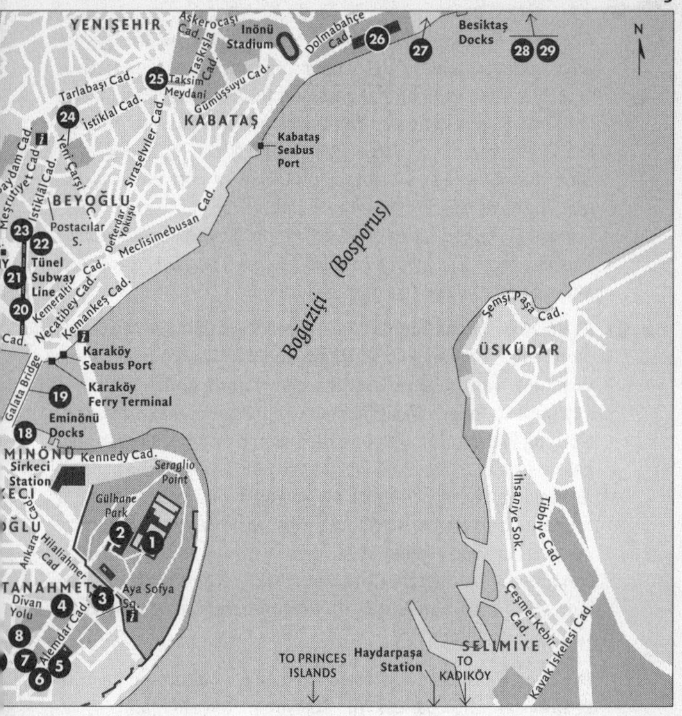

Stefi Stephan Bulgar Kilesi, 14

Süleymaniye Cami, 13

Taksim Meydanı, 25

Topkapı Sarayı, 1

Tünel Meydanı, 23

Voyvoda Caddesi, 20

Yerebatan Sarnıcı, 4

Yıldız Parkı, 29

treasures. The place needs a fresh coat of paint, the displays are unimaginative, and the descriptions of what you see are terse at best. The Tiled Pavilion has ceramics from the early Seljuk and Ottoman empires and tiles from İznik, which produced perhaps the finest ceramics in the world during the 17th and 18th centuries. Covered in a bright profusion of colored tiles, the building itself is part of the exhibit. *Gülhane Park, adjacent to Topkapı Palace, tel. 212/520–7740. $3 (total) for the 3 museums. Archaeology Museum: Tues.–Sun. 9:30–4:30; Tiled Pavilion: Tues.–Sun. 9:30–noon; Museum of the Ancient Orient: Tues.–Sun. 1–5.*

★ ❸ **AYA SOFYA** (Hagia Sophia). The magnificent dome of Aya Sofya, more commonly known as Hagia Sophia (Church of the Holy Wisdom), was the world's largest church from its completion in 537 until St. Peter's Basilica was built in Rome 1,000 years later. Nothing like the dome's construction had ever been attempted before—new architectural rules had to be made up as the builders went along. Perhaps the greatest work of Byzantine architecture, the cathedral was Christendom's most important church for 900 years. It survived earthquakes, looting crusaders, and the city's conquest by Mehmet the Conqueror in 1453. The church was then converted into a mosque; its four minarets were added by succeeding sultans.

The church's Byzantine mosaics were plastered over in the 16th century at the behest of Süleyman the Magnificent in accordance with the Islamic proscription against the portrayal of the human figure in a place of worship. In 1936 Atatürk made Aya Sofya into a museum. Shortly thereafter American archaeologists rediscovered the mosaics, which were restored and are now on display. Above where the altar once stood is a giant portrait of a somber Virgin Mary with the infant Jesus, and alongside are severe-looking depictions of archangels Michael and Gabriel.

Ascend to the gallery above, and you will find the best of the remaining mosaics, executed in the 13th century. There is a group with Emperor John Comnenus, the Empress Zoë and her husband (actually, her third husband; his face was added atop his predecessors'), and Jesus with Mary, and another of John the Baptist. According to legend, the marble-and-brass **Sacred Column** in the north aisle of the mosque weeps water that can work miracles. Over the centuries believers have worn a hole through the column with their constant caresses. Today visitors of many faiths stick their fingers in the hole and make a wish; nobody will mind if you do so as well. In recent years there has been growing pressure for Aya Sofya to be reopened for Muslim worship. Some people often gather to pray at the museum at midday on Friday. As with mosques, it is best not to try to visit then. *Aya Sofya Sq., tel. 212/522–1750. $4.50. Tues.–Sun. 9:30–4:30.*

NEED A BREAK? For a real treat, spend an hour in a Turkish bath. One of the best is **Cağaloğlu Hamamı** (Prof. Kazı Gürkan Cad. 34, Cağaloğlu, tel. 212/522–2424), in a magnificent 18th-century building near Aya Sofya. Florence Nightingale and Kaiser Wilhelm II once soaked here; the clientele today remains generally upscale (Turks of lesser means head for plainer, less costly baths). You are given a cubicle in which to strip down—and a towel to cover yourself with—and are then escorted into a steamy, marble-clad temple to cleanliness. Self-service baths cost just $10; an extra $5–$10 buys you that time-honored, punishing-yet-relaxing pummeling known as Turkish massage. The baths are open daily 8–8 for women and until 10 PM for men.

★ 5 **BLUE MOSQUE** (Sultan Ahmet Cami). This massive structure, officially called Sultan Ahmet Cami (Mosque of Sultan Ahmet), is studded with mini- and semidomes and surrounded by six minarets. This number briefly linked it with the Elharam Mosque in Mecca, until Sultan Ahmet I (ruled 1603–17) was forced to send his architect down to the Holy City to build a seventh minaret and reestablish Elharam's eminence. Press through the throng of people selling things, and enter the mosque at the side entrance that faces Aya Sofya. You must remove your shoes and leave them at the entrance. Immodest clothing is not allowed, but an attendant at the door will lend you a robe if he feels you are not dressed appropriately. Women should cover their heads.

Only after you enter the Blue Mosque do you understand why it is so named. Inside it is decorated with 20,000 shimmering blue Iznik tiles interspersed with 260 stained-glass windows; an airy arabesque pattern is painted on the ceiling. After the dark corners and stern, sour faces of the Byzantine mosaics in Aya Sofya, this light-filled mosque is positively uplifting. Architect Mehmet Aga, known as Sedefkar (Worker of Mother-of-Pearl), spent eight years getting the mosque just right, beginning in 1609. His goal, set by Sultan Ahmet, was to surpass Justinian's masterpiece, Aya Sofya—completed nearly 1,100 years earlier—and many believe he succeeded.

The **Hünkar Kasrı** (Carpet and Kilim museums), two good places to prepare yourself for dueling with modern-day carpet dealers, are in the stone-vaulted cellars of the Blue Mosque and upstairs at the end of a stone ramp, where the sultans rested before and after their prayers. Here rugs are treated as works of art and displayed in a suitably grand setting. *Sultanahmet Sq., tel. 212/518–1330 for museum information only. Mosque free; museums $1.50. Blue Mosque: daily 9–5, access restricted during prayer times, particularly at midday on Fri.; museums: weekdays 8:30–noon and 1–3:30.*

❼ **HIPPODROME.** Once a Byzantine stadium with seating for 100,000, the Hippodrome was the center for public entertainments such as chariot races and circuses. Disputes between rival groups of supporters of chariot teams often degenerated into violence. Thirty thousand people died here in what came to be known as the Nike riots of AD 531.

The original shape of the Hippodrome is still clearly visible. The monuments that can be seen today on the grassy open space opposite the Blue Mosque—the **Egyptian Obelisk** (Dikilitaş from the 15th century BC, the **Column of Constantinos** (Örme Sütün), and the **Serpentine Column** (Yılanlı Sütun), taken from the Temple of Apollo at Delphi in Greece—formed part of the central barrier around which the chariots raced. The Hippodrome was originally adorned with a life-size bronze sculpture of four horses. That piece was taken by the Venetians and can now be seen at the entrance to the Cathedral of San Marco in Venice. In this area you'll encounter hundreds of peddlers selling postcards, nuts, and souvenirs. *Atmeydanı, Sultanahmet. Free. Accessible at all hrs.*

★ 8 **IBRAHIM PAŞA SARAYI** (Ibrahim Paşa Palace). The grandiose residence of the son-in-law and grand vizier of Süleyman the Magnificent was built circa 1524. The striated stone mansion was outfitted by Süleyman to be the finest private residence in Istanbul, but Ibrahim Paşa didn't have long to enjoy it: He was executed when he became too powerful for the liking of Süleyman's power-crazed wife, Roxelana.

The palace now houses the **Türk Ve Islâm Eserleri Müzesi** (Museum of Turkish and Islamic Arts), where you can learn about the lifestyles of Turks at every level of society, from the 8th century to the present. *Atmeydanı 46, Sultanahmet, tel. 212/518–1385. $2. Tues.–Sun. 9–4:30.*

6 **MOZAIK MÜZESI** (Mosaic Museum). Tucked away behind the Blue Mosque, the often-overlooked Mosaic Museum is actually the ruins of the Great Palace of Byzantium, the imperial residence of the Byzantine emperors when they ruled lands stretching from Iran to Italy. The mosaics that give the museum its name lay hidden beneath the earth for 1,000 years before being uncovered by archaeologists in 1935. Scenes of animals, flowers, and trees in many of the mosaics depict rural idylls far removed from the pomp and elaborate ritual of the imperial court. *Arasta Çarşısı, Kabasakal Cad., Sultanahmet, tel. 212/518–1205. $1.50. Wed.–Mon. 9–4.*

9 **SOKOLLU MEHMET PAŞA CAMI** (Mosque of Mehmet Paşa). This small mosque, built in 1571, is generally regarded as one of the most beautifully realized projects of the master architect Sinan, who designed more than 350 other buildings and monuments under the direction of Süleyman the Magnificent. Rather than dazzle with size, he integrated all the parts into a harmonious whole, from the courtyard and porticoes outside to the delicately carved *minbar* (pulpit) and well-preserved İznik tiles set off by pure white walls and floral-motif stained-glass windows inside. *Mehmet Paşa Cad. at Özbekler Sok., Küçük Ayasofya, no phone. Free. Daily sunrise–sunset, except during prayer times.*

★ 1 **TOPKAPI SARAYI** (Topkapı Palace). Istanbul's number-one attraction sits on Seraglio Point, where the Bosporus meets the Golden Horn. The vast palace was the residence of sultans and their harems until 1868, when Sultan Abdül Mecit I (ruled 1839–61) moved to the European-style Dolmabahçe Palace farther up the Bosporus. The palace gates open at 9; plan to spend several hours and go early before the bus-tour crowds pour in. If you go by taxi, be sure to tell the driver you want the Topkapı Sarayı in Sultanahmet, or you could end up at the Topkapı bus terminal on the outskirts of town.

Sultan Mehmet II built the original palace during the 1450s, shortly after his conquest of Constantinople. Over the centuries, sultan after sultan added ever more elaborate architectural frills and fantasies, until the palace had acquired four courtyards and quarters for some 5,000 full-time residents, including slaves, concubines, and eunuchs.

The initial approach to the palace does little to evoke the many tales of intrigue, bloodshed, and drama attached to the structure. The first entrance, or Imperial Gate, leads to the **Court of the Janissaries,** also known as the First Courtyard, an area the size of a football field that now serves as a parking lot. As you walk ahead to the ticket office, look to your left, where you will see the **Aya Irini** (Church of St. Irene, Hagia Eirene in Greek). This unadorned redbrick building, now used for concerts, dates to the earliest days of Byzantium.

Formed in the 14th century as the sultan's corps of elite guards, the Janissaries were taken as young boys from non-Muslim families in Ottoman-controlled territories in the Balkans, taught Turkish, and instructed in Islam. Though theoretically the sultan's vassals, these professional soldiers quickly became a power in their own right, and more than once their protests culminated in the murder of the reigning sultan. During the rule of Sultan Mahmut II (ruled 1808–39), the tables were finally turned, and the Janissaries were massacred in what came to be known as the Auspicious Event.

Next to the ticket office is the **Bab-ı-Selam** (Gate of Salutation), built in 1524 by Süleyman the Magnificent, who was the only person allowed to pass through it on horseback; others had to dismount and enter on foot. Prisoners were kept in the towers on either side before their execution next to the nearby fountain. Once you pass this gate, you begin to experience the grandeur of the palace.

The **Second Courtyard,** just slightly smaller than the first, is planted with rose gardens and ornamental trees and filled with a series of ornate *köşks*, pavilions once used for both the business of state and for more mundane matters, like feeding the hordes of servants. To the right are the palace's immense kitchens, which now display one of the world's best collections of Chinese porcelain, including 10th-century T'ang, Yuan celadon, and Ming blue-and-white pieces dating from the 18th century, when the Chinese produced pieces to order for the palace.

Straight ahead is the **Divan-ı-Humayun** (Assembly Room of the Council of State), once presided over by the grand vizier. When the mood struck him, the sultan would sit behind a latticed

topkapı sarayı

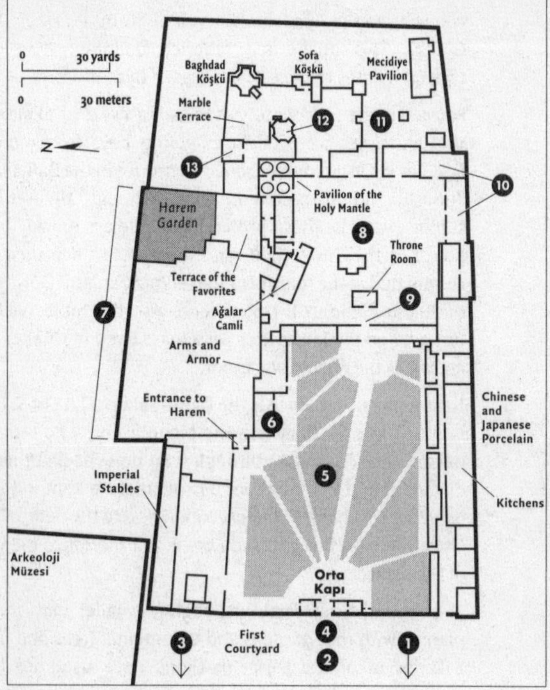

Imperial Gate, 1
Court of the Janissaries, 2
Aya Irini, 3
Bab-ı-Selam, 4
Second Courtyard, 5
Divan-ı-Humayun, 6
Harem, 7
Third Courtyard, 8
Bab-ı-Saadet, 9
Treasury, 10
Fourth Courtyard, 11
Rivan Köşkü, 12
Sünnet Odası, 13

window, hidden by a curtain, so no one would know when he was listening, although occasionally he would pull the curtain aside to comment.

One of the most popular sections of Topkapı is the **Harem,** a maze of 400 halls, terraces, rooms, wings, and apartments grouped around the sultan's private quarters to the west of the Second Courtyard. Only 40 rooms, all meticulously restored, are open to the public; they can be visited only on tours, which leave every half hour (and cost $1.50). These rooms illustrate both the opulence and the regimentation of harem life. Only a few of the resident concubines qualified for presentation to the sultan; of those, only the chosen walked the Golden Way, by which the favorite of the night entered the sultan's private quarters.

The first areas you see, which housed the palace eunuchs and about 200 lesser concubines, resemble a monastery; the tiny cubicles are as cramped and uncomfortable as the Harem's main rooms are large and opulent. Private apartments around a shared courtyard housed the chief wives (Islamic law permitted up to four); the *valide* sultan (queen mother), the absolute ruler of the Harem, had quite a bit of space as well as her own courtyard and marble bath. The sultan's private rooms are a riot of brocades, murals, colored marble, wildly ornate furniture, gold leaf, and fine carving. Fountains, also much in evidence, were not only decorative—they made it hard to eavesdrop on royal conversations. All told, it is a memorable, worthy backdrop to the rise and fall of princes and pretenders.

You exit the Harem into the somewhat smaller **Third Courtyard.** To see it best, make your way to its main gate, the **Bab-ı-Saadet** (Gate of Felicity), then exit and reenter. Shaded by regal old trees, the Third Courtyard is dotted by some of the most ornate of the palace's pavilions. Foreign ambassadors once groveled just past the gate in the **Arz Odası** (Audience Chamber), but access to the courtyard was highly restricted, in part because it housed the **Treasury,** four rooms filled with jewels, including two uncut emeralds, each weighing about 8 pounds, that once hung from the ceiling. Here, too, are the dazzling emerald dagger used in the movie *Topkapi* and the 84-carat Spoonmaker diamond, which, according to legend, was found by a pauper and traded for three wooden spoons. Not surprisingly, this is one of the most popular sections of the palace, and it can get quite crowded.

Also within this courtyard you can view a collection of thousands of Turkish and Persian miniatures, relics of the prophet Muhammad, and the rich costumes of the Imperial Wardrobe. Imperial fashion (male, of course) evolves slowly in the magnificent display of sultans' robes from the first to the last ruler. Some robes are bloodstained and torn from assassins' daggers; garments are stiff with gold and silver thread, tooled leather, and gold, silver, and jewels.

The **Fourth Courtyard,** the last, contains small, elegant summer houses, mosques, fountains, and reflecting pools scattered amid the gardens. Here you will find the cruciform **Rivan Köşkü,** built by Murat IV in 1636 to commemorate a military victory. In another pavilion, the **İftariye** (Golden Cage), the closest relatives of the reigning sultan lived in strict confinement under what amounted to house arrest, ostensibly to help keep the peace, although it meant that heirs had no opportunity to prepare themselves for the formidable task of ruling a great empire. The custom began during the 1800s, superseding an older practice of murdering all possible rivals to the throne.

Just off the open terrace with the wishing well is the lavishly tiled **Sünnet Odası** (Circumcision Room), where little princes would be taken for ritual circumcision during their 9th or 10th year. *Topkapı Palace, Gülhane Park, near Sultanahmet Sq., tel. 212/512–0480. $4, plus $2 for harem tour. Wed.–Mon. 9:30–4:30.*

NEED A BREAK? Just past the Topkapı Palace's Treasury, on the right side of the courtyard, are steps leading to the 19th-century rococo-style Mecidiye Pavilion, also known as the Köşk of Sultan Abdül Mecit I (ruled 1839–61), for whom it was built. It now houses the **Konyalı Restaurant** (tel. 212/513–9696), which serves traditional Turkish dishes (albeit with a mass-produced flavor) and has magnificent views. On a terrace below is an outdoor café with an even better view. Go early to beat the tour-group crush. The restaurant and the café are open for lunch only.

★ 4 **YEREBATAN SARNICI** (Sunken Cistern). Also known as the Basilica Cistern, Yerebatan Sarnıcı is the most impressive part of an underground network of waterways said to have been created at the behest of Emperor Constantine in the 4th century and expanded by Justinian in the 6th century (most of the present structure dates from the Justinian era). The cistern was always kept full as a precaution against long sieges. Today it is an atmospheric space, with 336 marble columns rising 26 ft to support Byzantine arches and domes. Piped-in classical music accompanies the sound of endlessly dripping water. *Yerebatan Cad. at Divan Yolu, tel. 212/522–1259. $3. Daily 9–4:30.*

OFF THE BEATEN PATH **KARIYE MÜZESI** – Often passed over because of its inconvenient location at Istanbul's western edge, near the remnants of the city's Byzantine walls, the Kariye Museum occupies what was once the Church of the Holy Savior in Chora, erected in the 5th century under the aegis of Justinian and rebuilt several times since. You come to see the dazzling 14th-century mosaics and frescoes depicting biblical scenes from Adam to the life of Christ; they are considered among the finest Byzantine works in the world. The historic Ottoman buildings around the museum have been restored as well. A tea shop on the garden terrace serves light fare.

Just west of the Chora are the Constantinian Walls, built by Emperor Theodosius II in AD 413. The massive walls, several stories high and from 10 ft to 20 ft thick in spots, protected Constantinople from onslaught after onslaught by Huns, Bulgarians, Russians, Arabs, Goths, and Turks. The walls were breached only twice: by the crusaders in the 1200s and by Mehmet the Conqueror in 1453. *1 block north of Fevzipaşa Cad., by Edirne Gate in city's outer walls, tel. 212/631–9241. $2. Thurs.–Tues. 9:30–4.*

GRAND BAZAAR TO EMINÖNÜ

This walk leads you through several markets, including two of Istanbul's largest, and takes you to two of the city's most beautiful mosques.

A Good Walk

After a visit to the **Grand Bazaar** ⑩, exit through the front entrance on Yeniçeriler Caddesi and head west to that street's junction with Çadırcı Camii Caddesi. You'll see **Beyazıt Cami** ⑪ as you turn right onto Çadırcı Camii Caddesi, which runs into Fuatpaşa Caddesi. Follow Fuatpaşa Caddesi along the eastern side of the grounds of **Istanbul University** ⑫. Continue along Fuatpaşa Caddesi, keeping the grounds of the university on your left, until the junction with Prof. Sıddık Sami Ona Caddesi and Ismetiye Caddesi. Turn left along Prof. Sıddık Sami Ona Caddesi to **Süleymaniye Cami** ⑬.

After visiting this mosque, retrace your steps along Prof. Sıddık Sami Ona Caddesi, continue straight across into Ismetiye Caddesi, and then turn left down Çarsı Caddesi. Along the narrow road leading downhill is a thriving market lined with stalls and small shops selling mostly cheap clothing. Continue down the hill to Hasırcılar Caddesi to head into the **Eminönü** ⑱ neighborhood. The **Rüstem Paşa Cami** ⑯ is at the western edge of this neighborhood. After visiting this mosque, continue along Hasırcılar Caddesi to the **Egyptian Bazaar** ⑰.

TIMING

Not counting the time you can spend exploring the Grand Bazaar, it takes about an hour to complete this walk. If you spend a brief amount of time in each of the mosques and bazaars and stop for lunch, then it will take you about four or five hours. The Grand and Egyptian bazaars are closed Sunday, though the small Arasta Bazaar, in the Sultanahmet neighborhood, is open. The Beyazıt, Rüstem Paşa, and Süleymaniye mosques are open daily.

Sights to See

11 **BEYAZIT CAMI.** This domed mosque, inspired by Aya Sofya, dates from 1504 and is the oldest of the Ottoman imperial mosques still standing in the city. *Beyazıt Meyd., Beyazıt, no phone. Free. Daily, sunrise to sunset; usually closed during prayer times.*

★ 17 **EGYPTIAN BAZAAR** (Mısır Çarşısı). Also known as the Spice Market, the Egyptian Bazaar is much smaller than the Grand Bazaar but is still lively and colorful. It was built in the 17th century to generate rental income to pay for the upkeep of the **Yeni Cami** (New Mosque), next door. Once a vast pharmacy filled with burlap bags overflowing with herbs and spices, the bazaar today is chockablock with white sacks of spices, as well as bags full of fruit, nuts, and royal jelly from the beehives of the Aegean Sea. *Hamidiye Cad., across from Galata Bridge, no phone. Mon.–Sat. 8–7.*

NEED A BREAK? The **Pandelli,** up two flights of stairs over the arched gateway to the Egyptian Bazaar, is a frenetic Old Istanbul restaurant with impressive tile work. A lunch of typical Turkish fare is served; especially good are the eggplant *börek* (pastry) and the sea bass cooked in paper. *Mısır Çarşısı 1, Eminönü, tel. 212/527–3909. AE, MC, V.*

18 **EMINÖNÜ.** The main transportation hub of Old Stamboul, Eminönü, is a neighborhood at the south end of the Galata

Bridge. It has quays for hydrofoil sea buses, the more traditional Bosporus ferries (including those for the daylong Bosporus cruises), and the Sirkeci train station and tramway terminal. The main coastal road around the peninsula of the old city also traverses Eminönü. Thousands of people and vehicles rush through the bustling area, and numerous street traders here sell everything from candles to live animals.

15 **EYÜP CAMII.** The mosque complex at Eyüp on the Golden Horn houses the tomb of Eyüp Ensari, the Prophet Muhammad's standard-bearer, who was killed during the first Arab siege, AD 674–78, of what was then Constantinople. Most of the original complex was built in the 15th century by Sultan Mehmet the Conqueror. It was added to by his successors and numerous Ottoman dignitaries, many of whom, including several sultans' wives, had their own tombs built close by.

Today Eyüp is the holiest Islamic shrine in Turkey and attracts Muslim pilgrims from all over the world. Despite the numbers, particularly at Friday midday prayer, the plane-tree-shaded courtyards and hundreds of fluttering pigeons imbue it with a sense of peace and religious devotion not found anywhere else in this often frenetic city. The tomb itself is small and covered with brightly decorated ceramic tiles. Non-Muslims are welcome to join the hushed pilgrims who go to pray at the tomb but should remember to remove their shoes beforehand; women must be modestly dressed and must cover their heads before entering. *Camii Kebir Caddesi, Eyüp, no phone. Daily.*

★ 10 **GRAND BAZAAR** (Kapalı Çarşı). This early version of a shopping mall, also known as the Covered Bazaar, consists of a maze of 65 winding, covered streets crammed with 4,000 tiny shops, cafés, and restaurants. It reputedly has the largest number of stores under one roof anywhere in the world. Originally built by Mehmet II (the Conqueror) in the 1450s, it was ravaged in modern times by two fires—one in 1954 that nearly destroyed it, and a smaller one in

1974. In both cases, the bazaar was quickly rebuilt into something resembling the original style, with arched passageways and brass-and-tile fountains at regular intervals.

The Grand Bazaar is filled with thousands of items—fabric, clothing (including counterfeit brand names), brass candelabra, furniture, and jewelry. A sizable share of junk tailored for the tourist trade is sold as well. A separate section for antiques at the very center of the bazaar, called the **bedestan**, always has worthwhile offerings. Outside the western gate to the bazaar, through a doorway, is the **Sahaflar Çarşısı,** the Old Book Bazaar, where you can buy both new editions and antique volumes in Turkish and other languages. The best way to explore the bazaar is to take a deep breath and plunge on in. And remember: The best prices are those called out to you when the would-be seller thinks you are about to slip away. *Yeniçeriler Cad. and Fuatpaş a Cad. Free. Apr.–Oct., Mon.–Sat. 8:30–7; Nov.–Mar., Mon.–Sat. 8:30–6:30.*

12 **ISTANBUL UNIVERSITY.** The university's magnificent gateway faces Beyazıt Square. The campus, with its long greensward and giant plane trees, originally served as the Ottoman war ministry, which helps explain the grandiose, martial style of the portal and the main buildings. In the garden stands the white-marble 200-ft **Beyazıt Tower,** the tallest structure in Old Stamboul, built in 1823 by Mahmut II (ruled 1808–39) as a fire-watch station. *Fuat Paşa Cad., Beyazıt.*

16 **RÜSTEM PAŞA CAMI** (Rüstem Paşa Mosque). This small and often overlooked mosque is another Sinan masterpiece. Tucked away in the backstreets to the north of the Egyptian Bazaar, it was built in the 1550s for Süleyman's grand vizier. Though unassuming from the outside, its interior is decorated with Iznik tiles in an array of colors and patterns. *Hasırcılar Cad., south of Sobacılar Cad., no phone. Daily.*

13 **SÜLEYMANIYE CAMI** (Mosque of Süleyman). The grandest and most famous creation of its designer, Sinan, this mosque houses his

tomb and that of his patron, Süleyman the Magnificent. Its enormous dome is supported by four square columns and arches, and exterior walls buttress smaller domes on either side. The result is a soaring space that gives the impression the dome is held up principally by divine cooperation. This is the city's largest mosque, and it is both less ornate and more spiritual in tone than other imperial mosques. Note the İznik tiles in the *mihrab* (prayer niche). *Süleymaniye Cad., near Istanbul University's north gate, no phone. Daily.*

⑭ **STEFI STEFAN BULGAR KILESI** (Bulgarian Church of St. Stefan) is one of the most remarkable structures in Istanbul. Both the exterior and all the interior decor of this Neo-Gothic church, including what look to be carvings, are made entirely of cast iron. It was prefabricated in Vienna, shipped down the Danube, and erected on the western shore of the Golden Horn in 1871 by the then-flourishing Bulgarian Orthodox community in Istanbul, which was anxious to have an impressive church of its own to back its demand for independence from the Greek Orthodox patriarchate. Despite the dwindling numbers of the Bulgarian community, which means that there is not always someone on hand to unlock the interior, the church has been recently restored and repainted and is set in neatly tended gardens. *Mürsel Paşa Caddesi, Balat, no phone. Daily.*

GALATA TO TAKSIM

This walk covers the heart of the new town, where the first thing you'll learn is that *new* is a relative term. Much of what you'll see dates from the 19th century—except for the shops and imported American movies, which are all strictly contemporary. You can take the tiny subway up Karaköy to Tünel Square; only 90 seconds long, the trip spares you a stiff walk.

A Good Walk

Cross over the **Galata Köprüsü** ⑲, stopping on the bridge to take in one of the world's great city views. Continue due north

24 **GALATASARAY MEYDANI** (Galatasaray Square). This square is in the heart of the Beyoğlu district. The impressive building behind the massive iron gates on the square is a high school, established in 1868 and for a time the most prestigious in the Ottoman Empire.

Across İstiklal Caddesi, at Number 51, is the entrance to the **Çiçek Pasajı** (Flower Arcade), a lively warren of flower stalls, tiny restaurants, and bars. Street musicians often entertain here. Curmudgeons swear the passage is a pale shadow of its former self—its original neobaroque home collapsed with a thundering crash one night in 1978, and its redone facade and interior feel too much like a reproduction—but you can still get a feel for its bohemian past.

Behind the Flower Arcade is the **Balık Pazarı** (Fish Market), a bustling labyrinth of stands peddling fish, fruits, vegetables, and spices—with a couple of pastry shops thrown in—all of which makes for great street theater. The fish market is open from Monday through Saturday during daylight hours. At the end of the market, at Meşrutiyet Caddesi, is the **Üç Horan Armenian Church** (İstiklal Cad. 288). With its crosses and haloed Christs, the church is an unexpected sight in Muslim Istanbul.

İstiklal Caddesi (Independence Street). One of European Istanbul's main thoroughfares heads north and east to Taksim Square from Tünel Square. Consulates in ornate turn-of-the-century buildings and 19th-century apartments line the route, along with bookstores, boutiques, kebab shops, and movie theaters. To appreciate the architecture, look toward the upper stories of what was once the most fashionable street in the entire region. Return your gaze to eye level, and you will see every element of modern Istanbul's vibrant cultural melting pot. A trolley runs along İstiklal every 10 minutes or so, all the way to Taksim Square. The fare is about 50¢. If you have the time and energy, walk one way and take the trolley back.

25 **TAKSIM MEYDANI** (Taksim Square). This square at the north end of İstiklal Caddesi is in the not particularly handsome center of the new town, especially since municipal subway digging has recently turned its belly into a deep concrete crevasse. It's basically a chaotic traffic circle with a bit of grass and the **Monument to the Republic and Independence,** featuring Atatürk and his revolutionary cohorts.

Around the square are Istanbul's main concert hall, **Atatürk Kültür Merkezi** (Atatürk Cultural Center), the high-rise Marmara Hotel, and, on a grassy promenade, the 23-story Ceylan Inter-Continental (☞ Where to Stay). On **Cumhuriyet Caddesi,** the main street heading north from the square, are shops selling carpets and leather goods. Also here are the entrances to the Hyatt, Divan, and Istanbul Hilton hotels; several travel agencies and airline ticket offices; and a few nightclubs. Cumhuriyet turns into Halâskârgazi Caddesi. When this street meets Rumeli Caddesi, you enter the city's high-fashion district, where Turkey's top designers sell their wares.

NEED A BREAK? The **Patisserie Café Marmara,** in the Marmara Hotel on Taksim Square, serves hot and cold drinks and snacks, ice cream, and excellent homemade cakes. Despite the turbulence and often downright chaos of Taksim Square itself, the café retains an air of unhurried calm. A duo usually plays soothing classical music in the late afternoon and early evening. In summer the shaded terrace is a good place to observe the bustle of the square. *Marmara Istanbul, Taksim Sq., tel. 212/251–4696. AE, DC, MC, V.*

23 **TÜNEL MEYDANI** (Tünel Square). The northern terminus of the city's minisubway is at this square on the south end of İstiklal Caddesi. Nearby is the **Pera Palace,** one of the most famous of Istanbul's hotels, where Agatha Christie wrote *Murder on the Orient Express* and where Mata Hari threw back a few at the bar.

20 **VOYVODA CADDESI.** Considering all the romance that surrounds the 15th-century *voyvode* (prince) of Transylvania, Vlad the Impaler—better known as Count Dracula—it's a tad ironic that the street named after him is a nondescript commercial strip. As a child, Vlad was sent to the Ottoman sultan as ransom, and though he was finally released, he grew up despising the Turks. He devised elaborate tortures for his enemies and at length drove the Turks from Romania. Killed near Bucharest in 1476, his head was sent to Constantinople, where Mehmet II the Conqueror displayed it on a stake to prove to all that the hated Vlad was finally dead. Some say the street is the site of his grave.

OFF THE BEATEN PATH **RAHMI KOÇ SANAYI MÜZESI.** A restored foundry once used to cast anchors for the Ottoman fleet now houses this industrial museum tracing the development of technology. Exhibits include medieval telescopes and some well-crafted maritime instruments. A special section devoted to transportation includes planes, bicycles, motorbikes and the great engines that powered the Bosporus ferries. *27 Hasköy Cad., Hasköy, tel. 212/256–7153 or 212/256–7154, fax 212/256–7156. $1.50. Tues.–Sun. 10–4:30.*

BEŞIKTAŞ

The shore of the Bosporus became the favorite residence of the later Ottoman sultans as they sought to escape overcrowded Old Stamboul. They remained here until the end of the empire when eventually they, too, were engulfed by the ever-expanding city and, one could argue, by history as well.

A Good Walk

Start at the extravagant 19th-century **Dolmabahçe Sarayı** 26, the palace where the last sultans of the Ottoman Empire resided and where Atatürk lived. Exiting the palace, continue northeast along tree-lined Dolmabahçe Caddesi onto Beşiktaş Caddesi, site of the **Deniz Müzesi** ㉗, to get a sense of the Ottoman Empire's former naval power.

From here follow the main coast road past the Beşiktaş ferry terminal into Çırağan Caddesi and the **Çırağan Sarayı** ㉘, former home of the Sultan Abdül Aziz and now a luxury hotel. Directly opposite the hotel's main door is the entrance to the wooded slopes of **Yıldız Parkı** ㉙, probably the most romantic spot in Istanbul. Follow the road up the hill through the park and take a right at the top of the slope to get to Yıldız Şale, the chalet of the last of the Ottoman sultans.

TIMING

Allow approximately two hours for the walk from Dolmabahçe Sarayı to the entrance to Yıldız Parkı, including 45 minutes in the Deniz Müzesi (Naval Museum) and 30 minutes in the Çırağan Sarayı. Allow another two to three hours to walk through Yıldız Parkı—it has numerous trails—and include 45 minutes to an hour to visit Yıldız Şale. Dolmabahçe Sarayı is closed Monday and Thursday, and the Naval Museum Monday and Thursday. Yıldız Parkı is open daily, but Yıldız Şale is closed Monday and Tuesday.

Sights to See

㉘ **ÇIRAGAN SARAYI** (Çırağan Palace). Istanbul's most luxurious hotel (☞ Where to Stay) was built by Abdül Mecit's brother and successor, Sultan Abdül Aziz (ruled 1861–76), in 1863. That the palace is about a third the size of Dolmabahçe and much less ornate says a good deal about the declining state of the Ottoman Empire's coffers. The vacuous Abdül Aziz was as extravagant as his brother and was soon attempting to emulate the splendors he had seen on travels in England and France.

Today the restored grounds, with a splendid swimming pool at the edge of the Bosporus, are worth a look, and the hotel bar provides a plush, cool respite with a view. You won't find much from the original palace, as a major fire gutted the place; the lobby renovations were done with a nod to the palace's original 19th-century design, though the color scheme is decidedly gaudier. *Çırağan Cad. 84, Beşiktaş, tel. 212/258–3377.*

27 **DENIZ MÜZESI** (Naval Museum). The Ottoman Empire was the 16th century's leading sea power. The flashiest displays here are the sultan's barges, the long, slim boats that served as the primary mode of royal transportation for several hundred years. The museum's cannon collection includes a 23-ton blaster built for Sultan Selim the Grim. An early Ottoman map of the New World, cribbed from Columbus, dates from 1513. *Beşiktaş Cad., tel. 212/261–0040 or 212/261–0130. $1. Wed.–Sun. 9–12:30 and 1:30–5:30.*

26 **DOLMABAHÇE SARAYI** (Dolmabahçe Palace). The last sultans of the Ottoman Empire resided at this palace, erected in 1853. After the establishment of the modern republic in 1923, it became the home of Atatürk, who died here in 1938. The name, which means "filled-in garden," predates the palace; Sultan Ahmet I (ruled 1603–17) had an imperial garden planted here in the 17th century.

The palace is an extraordinary mixture of Hindu, Turkish, and European styles of architecture and interior design. Abdül Mecit, whose free-spending lifestyle (his main distinction) eventually bankrupted his empire, intended the structure to be a symbol of Turkey's march away from its past and toward the European mainstream. He gave his Armenian architect, Balian, complete freedom and an unlimited budget. His only demand was that the palace "surpass any other palace of any other potentate anywhere in the world."

The result was a riot of rococo—marble, vast mirrors, stately towers, and formal gardens along a facade stretching nearly ½ km (⅓ mi). His bed is solid silver; the tub and basins in his marble-paved bathroom are carved of translucent alabaster. Europe's royalty contributed to the splendor: Queen Victoria sent a chandelier weighing 4½ tons, Czar Nicholas I of Russia provided polar-bear rugs. The result is as gaudy and showy as a palace should be, all gilt and crystal and silk, and every bit as garish as Versailles. The nearby **Dolmabahçe Cami** (Dolmabahçe Mosque) was founded in 1853 by Abdül Mecit's mother. You must join a guided tour—one takes about 80 minutes, and another, which omits the harem, takes about 45 minutes. *Dolmabahçe Cad., tel. 212/258–5544. $10 for long tour, $5.50 for short tour. Tues.–Wed. and Fri.–Sun. 9–4.*

29 **YILDIZ PARKI.** The wooded slopes of Yıldız Park once formed part of the great forest that covered the European shore of the Bosporus from the Golden Horn to the Black Sea. During the reign of Abdül Aziz, the park was his private garden, and the women of the harem would occasionally be allowed to visit. First the gardeners would be removed, then the eunuchs would lead the women across the wooden bridge from the palace and along the avenue to the upper gardens. Secluded from prying eyes, they would sit in the shade or wander through the acacias, maples, and cypresses, filling their baskets with flowers and figs. Today the park is still hauntingly beautiful, particularly in spring and fall.

Yıldız Şale (Yıldız Chalet), at the top of the park, is yet another palace of Sultan Abdül Hamit II (ruled 1876–1909). Visiting dignitaries from Kaiser Wilhelm to Charles de Gaulle and Margaret Thatcher have stayed here. The chalet is often blissfully empty of other tourists, which makes a visit all the more pleasurable. Forgotten is the turmoil of the era when the palace was occupied by the last rulers of the once-great Ottoman Empire. All were deposed: free-spending Abdül Aziz; his unfortunate nephew, Murad (who, having spent most of his life in the Harem, was none too sound of mind); and Abdül Hamid, who distinguished himself as the last despot of the Ottoman Empire. *Çırağan Cad., tel. 212/261–8460 for park; 212/259–4570 for chalet. Park: 25¢ pedestrians, $1.50 cars; chalet: $1.50. Park: daily 9–9; chalet: Wed.–Sun. 9–4.*

★ The **Askeri Müze** (Military Museum), in the northwestern corner of the park, contains a fascinating collection of military memorabilia from the 15th century to the present. In addition to costumes, flags, and weapons—from swords and pistols to mighty cannons—the museum also houses some beautifully embroidered silk tents used by the Ottoman sultans on campaigns, personal artifacts belonging to Atatürk from the 1915 Gallipoli campaign, and even fragments of the great chain that the last Byzantine rulers of the Istanbul stretched across the Golden Horn in a vain attempt to prevent the Turks from gaining access to the city by sea. A *Mehter* (Janissary) military band performs 17th- and 18th-century Ottoman military music in full period costume on the grounds of the museum at 3 Wed–Sun during the summer. *Valikonağı Caddesi, Harbiye, tel. 212/233–2720.* $2. *Wed-Sun 9–5.*

THE BOSPORUS

Though there are good roads along both the Asian and the European shores, the most pleasant way to explore the Bosporus is by ferry from the Eminönü docks in the old town (☞ Boat & Ferry Travel *in* Practical Information). Along the way you will see wooded hills, villages large and small, modern and old-fashioned, and the old wooden summer homes called *yalıs* (waterside houses) that were built for the city's wealthier residents in the Ottoman era. When looking at ferry schedules, remember that Rumeli refers to the European side, Anadolu to the Asian.

A Good Ferry Tour

There are two ways to take a ferry tour of the Bosporus. One is to take one of the cruises that depart daily from Eminönü. These leave from Quay 3 (look for the sign BOĞAZ HATTI) at 10:35 and 1:35 (times are subject to change, so check first). The round-trip should cost about $2. The boats zigzag up the Bosporus, stop for a couple of hours near the Black Sea for lunch, then zigzag back down to Eminönü.

The other way is to fashion your own tour, hopping on one of the regular Bosporus commuter ferries, stopping wherever you fancy, and then continuing your journey on the next ferry going your way. (Buy a ferry timetable—a *vapur tarifesi*—to figure out your itinerary.) The advantage of the latter is more freedom; the disadvantage is that you will probably end up spending considerable extra time waiting for the next ferry. Note, too, that not all ferries stop at every quay along the Bosporus, and during the middle of the day schedules can be erratic.

After departing from Eminönü, the ferry heads north out of the Golden Horn and past the Dolmabahçe and Çırağan palaces on the European shore. As you approach the first Bosporus bridge you pass Ortaköy Cami (Ortaköy Mosque), on the European shore, and just past the bridge on the Asian shore, the **Beylerbeyi Sarayı** ㉚.

Back on the European side is the village of **Arnavutköy** ㉛, followed by the stylish suburb of **Bebek** ㉜. Just before the second Bosporus bridge (officially known as Fatih Sultan Mehmet Bridge) are two fortresses, **Anadolu Hisarı** ㉝, on the Asian side, and **Rumeli Hisarı** ㉞, on the European side. North of Fatih Sultan Mehmet Bridge, on the Asian side, lies the village of **Kanlıca** ㉟. Across the water are the wooded slopes of **Emirgan** ㊱. Still farther north on the European side are the fashionable resort area of Tarabya and the waterfront village of Sarıyer, the ferry stop for the **Sadberk Hanım Müzesi** ㊲, with its collection of Islamic and Turkish arts and Anatolian archaeological finds.

Organized cruises from Eminönü usually stop at either Rumeli Kavağı or Anadolu Kavağı, two fishing villages, for a couple of hours. Anadolu Kavağı is particularly fun; its sidewalk vendors sell deep-fried mussels and sweet waffles. The ferries begin their return trips to Istanbul from Rumeli Kavağı and Anadolu Kavağı.

TIMING

Whether you take a Bosporus cruise or make your own way by ferry, you should allow a whole day. The cruises usually take about six hours. If you don't opt for a cruise, add at least an extra hour (if not longer) waiting for ferries in addition to the time spent at stops along the way. Rumeli Hisarı is closed Monday. Beylerbeyi Sarayı is closed Monday and Thursday. Sadberk Hanım Müzesi is closed Wednesday.

Sights to See

33 **ANADOLU HISARI** (Anatolian Castle). Sultan Beyazıt I built this fortress in 1393 to cut off Constantinople's access to the Black Sea. At the mouth of the Göksu stream, known in Ottoman times as one of the "Sweet Waters of Asia," the castle is a romantic sight (especially at sunset). Its golden stone blends into the surrounding forest, and tiny boats bob beneath its walls (some of which are crumbling, so be careful if walking on them. An unmarked path leads up to the castle ruins; there's no admission fee.

31 **ARNAVUTKÖY.** This village on the European side of the Bosporus has a row of 19th-century wooden houses at the water's edge. Up the hill from the water, narrow streets contain more old wooden houses, some of them with trailing vines.

32 **BEBEK.** One of the most fashionable suburbs of Istanbul, particularly with an affluent expatriate community, Bebek has a shaded park on the waterfront next to the mosque, good restaurants and open-air cafés, and a jazz club. Small rowing boats and even sizable cutters with crew can be rented for trips around Bebek Bay.

30 **BEYLERBEYI SARAYI** (Beylerbeyi Palace). Built for Sultan Abdül Aziz in 1865, Beylerbeyi is a mini-Dolmabahçe, filled with marble and marquetry and gold-encrusted furniture. The central hall has a white-marble fountain and a stairway wide enough for a

the bosporus

TO KILYOS
Rumeli Kavağı
Bahçeköy
BELGRADE FOREST
Sarıyer
Anadolu Kavağı
Sadberk Hanım Müzesi 37
Büyükdere
Kefeliköy
N
2 miles
0
3 km
Yalıköy
Tarabya
Beykoz
Yeniköy
Paşabahçe
Ayazaga
İstinye
Maslak
Boyacıköy
Emirgan 36
Çubuklu
TEM E80
35 Kanlıca
Fatih Sultan Mehmet Bridge
Rumelihisari
34
Rumeli Hisarı
Anadoluhisarı
Bosporus (Boğaziçi)
33 Anadolu Hisarı
Bebek 32
Kandilli
Arnavutköy 31
E80/100
Vaniköy
Çengelköy
Ortaköy Cami
Ortaköy
Beşiktaş
30 Beylerbeyi Sarayı
TO ISTANBUL
Dolmabahçe Sarayı
Bosporus Bridge
BEYOĞLU

regiment. You must join a tour to see the palace. *Çayıbaşı Durağı, Beylerbeyi, tel. 216/321–9320. $3. Tues.–Wed. and Fri.–Sun. 9:30–5.*

36 **EMIRGAN.** This town on the European shore of the Bosporus was named after a 17th-century Persian prince to whom Sultan Murat IV (ruled 1623–40) presented a palace here. The woods above are part of a park with flower gardens and a number of restored Ottoman pavilions. In late April the town stages a Tulip Festival. These flowers take their name from the Turkish *tulbend* (turban); the flowers were originally brought from Mongolia, and after their cultivation was refined by the Dutch, they were great favorites of the Ottoman sultans.

35 **KANLICA.** White 19th-century wooden villas line the waterfront of this village on the Asian shore. Kanlıca has been famous for its delicious yogurt for at least 300 years; it's served in little restaurants around the plane tree in the square by the quay.

34 **RUMELI HISARI** (Thracian Castle). Mehmet the Conqueror built this eccentric-looking fortress in 1452, a year before his siege of Constantinople finally succeeded. Its crenellated walls and round towers are popular with photographers, though what you view from the water is about all there is to see. In summer Rumeli Hisarı is sometimes used for Shakespeare performances (usually in Turkish) and music and folk dancing. *Rumeli Hisarı Cad., no phone. $1. Tues.–Sun. 9:30–5.*

37 **SADBERK HANIM MÜZESI** (Sadberk Hanım Museum). An old waterfront mansion houses this museum named for the deceased wife of the late billionaire businessman Vehbi Koç. Though small, it houses an enviable collection of high-quality pieces. Half the museum is dedicated to Islamic and Turkish arts (from İznik tiles to Ottoman embroidery and calligraphy), and half to Anatolian archaeology (Hittite pottery and cuneiform tablets). *Piyasa Cad. 27–29, Büyükdere, tel. 212/242–3813. $2. Apr.–Oct., Thurs.–Tues. 10:30–6; Nov.–Mar., Thurs.–Tues. 10–5.*

In This Chapter

Updated by Gareth Jenkins

eating out

TURKISH CUISINE IS FULL OF VEGETABLES, grains, fresh fish, and seemingly infinite varieties of lamb. Fish and meat are typically served grilled or roasted, although often with inordinate amounts of *yağ* (oil). The core group of seasonings is garlic, sage, oregano, cumin, mint, dill, lemon, and yogurt, always more yogurt. Turkish yogurt is among the tastiest in the world: Many travelers swear it helps keep their stomachs calm and stable while on the road.

Breakfast, usually eaten at your hotel, typically consists of *beyaz peynir* (goat cheese), sliced tomatoes, cucumbers, and olives, with a side order of fresh bread; the menu varies little, whether you stay in a simple pansiyon or an upscale hotel. Yogurt with honey and fresh fruit is generally available as well, as are tea and coffee.

Mezes, or appetizers, come in many varieties and are brought to your table with a basket of bread. Standard cold mezes include *patlıcan salatası* (roasted eggplant puree flavored with garlic and lemon), *haydarı* (a thick yogurt dip made with garlic and dill), *dolma* (stuffed grape leaves, peppers, or mussels), *ezme* (a spicy paste of tomatoes, minced green pepper, onion, and parsley), *kızartma* (deep-fried eggplant, zucchini, or green pepper served with fresh yogurt), *cacık* (a garlicky cold yogurt "soup" with shredded cucumber, mint, or dill), *barbunya pilaki* (kidney beans, tomatoes, and onions cooked in olive oil), and *barbunya pilaki* (slow-roasted baby eggplant topped with olive oil–fried onions and tomatoes and seasoned with garlic). One taste of this last meze, and you'll understand how it got its name—

which means, "The imam fainted with delight." Inevitably there will be other dishes based on eggplant, *patlıcan* in Turkish. Hot appetizers, usually called *ara sıcak*, include *börek* (a deep-fried or oven-baked pastry filled with cheese or meat), *kalamar* (deep-fried calamari served with a special sauce), and *midye tava* (deep-fried mussels).

Available almost any place you stop to eat, kebabs (*kebaps* in Turkish) come in many guises. Although the ingredient of choice for Turks is lamb, some kebabs are made with beef, chicken, or fish, usually grilled with vegetables on a skewer. *Adana kebaps* are spicy ground-lamb patties arranged on a layer of sautéed pita bread, topped with a zippy yogurt-and-garlic sauce. *İskender kebaps*, also known as *Bursa kebaps*, are sliced grilled lamb, smothered in tomato sauce, hot butter, and yogurt. *Şiş kebaps* are the traditional skewered cubes of lamb, usually interspersed with peppers and onions. *Köfte kebaps* are meatballs made from minced lamb mixed with rice, bulgur, or bread crumbs, then threaded onto skewers.

Fresh fish, often a main course, is commonly served grilled and drizzled with olive oil and lemon. You will find *alabalık* (trout), *barbunya* (red mullet), *kalkan* (turbot), *kefal* (gray mullet), *kılıç* (swordfish, sometimes served as a kebab), *levrek* (sea bass), *lüfer* (bluefish), and *palamut* (bonito).

In the meat department, there is *mantı*, a sort of Turkish ravioli served with garlicky yogurt that has a touch of mint. Grilled quail is most common inland; it's often marinated in tomatoes, yogurt, olive oil, and cinnamon. *Karışık ızgara*, a mixed grill, usually combines tender chicken breast, beef, a lamb chop, and spicy lamb patties, all served with rice pilaf and vegetables. *Tandır kebap*, lamb cooked in a pit, is a typical Anatolian dish.

As for desserts, you'll encounter several varieties of *baklava* (phyllo pastry with honey and chopped nuts) and *burma kadayıf* (shredded wheat in honey or syrup). Also popular are puddings, made of yogurt and eggs, and sweet rice or milk and rice flour.

Alcohol is readily available and widely consumed, despite Turkey's predominantly Muslim culture. Among the perfectly acceptable, inexpensive local wines, the best are Villa Doluca and Kavaklidere, available in *beyaz* (white) and *kırmızı* (red). The most popular local beer is Efes Pilsen, your basic American-type pilsner. In late 1997 Efes also started making a black beer called Efes Dark, and Tuborg pilsner is brewed under license in Turkey. In upscale bars and hotels it is also sometimes possible to find imported beers such as Budweiser.

The national drink is *rakı*, a relative of the Greek ouzo, made from grapes and aniseed. Usually it's mixed with water or ice, though many connoisseurs insist that it's best drunk neat, with each sip of rakı followed immediately by a sip of cold water. People drink it throughout their meal or as an aperitif.

Istanbul has a range of restaurants—and prices to match. Most major hotels serve standard international cuisine, so it's more rewarding to eat in Turkish restaurants. In addition to the ubiquitous kebabs, Istanbul is also famous for its fish, although it is wise to check prices and ask what is in season before ordering. Dress is casual unless otherwise noted.

The simplest establishments, Turkey's fast-food joints, are the *kebapçı*, the *dönerçı*, and the *pideçı*. The first specializes in kebabs. Dönerçıs provide a quick meal of spicy, spit-roasted sliced lamb, served either as a sandwich or with rice. At the pideçı, you'll find *pide*, a pizzalike snack made of flat bread topped with either butter, cheese, and egg or ground lamb and baked in a wood-fired oven. Often these eateries are little more than counters at which you belly up to the bar for instant gratification; on occasion they attain luncheonette status.

Lokantas are unpretentious neighborhood spots that make up the vast majority of Turkish restaurants. Lokantas are frequently open-air, the better to take advantage of the waterfront and sky, or are surrounded by flower-filled trellises. Often you serve yourself cafeteria style from big display cases full of hot and cold dishes—a relief if you don't speak Turkish. If there is no menu, it is because the chef only serves what is fresh, and that changes from day to day.

In the more upscale *restorans* (restaurants), you can expect tablecloths, menus, even a wine list, and dishes drawn from the richer, "palace" cuisine of Turkish royalty, often with Continental touches.

Prices in the restaurant chart below are per person and include an appetizer, main course, and dessert but not drinks and gratuities. A service charge of 10% to 15% is added to the bill; waiters expect another 10%. If a restaurant's menu has no prices listed, ask before you order—you'll avoid a surprise when the bill comes.

CATEGORY	ISTANBUL	OTHER AREAS
$$$$	over $40	over $30
$$$	$25–$40	$20–$30
$$	$12–$25	$10–$20
$	under $12	under $10

ASIAN SHORE

$$$$ **REŞAT PAŞA KONAĞI.** A chic atmosphere prevails inside this pink-and-white gingerbread-style villa. It's a little out of the way, on the Asian side, but the delicious Ottoman and Turkish dishes are well worth the trip (which you can make with a taxi driver instructed by someone at your hotel). Order à la carte and sample the mixed seafood cooked in a clay pot, or let the waiter tempt you with the Paşa Sofrasi, a fixed-price menu that includes 20 cold and hot appetizers, shish kebab as a main course, and lemon *helva* (halvah) for dessert, all accompanied by unlimited domestic drinks. A band plays *fasil* (traditional Turkish music) on weekends. *Sinan Ercan Cad. 34/1, Kozyatağı Mah., Erenköy, tel. 216/361–3411 or 216/361–3487. AE, DC, V. Closed Mon. No lunch.*

SOUTH OF THE GOLDEN HORN

$$$ **DEVELI RESTAURANT.** One of the oldest and best kebab ★ restaurants in Istanbul also has great views across the Sea of Marmara. The specialty is dishes from southeast Anatolia, which are traditionally more spicy than those in the west of the country. Try the *patlıcan kebap* (kebab with eggplant) or the *fıstıklı kebap* (kebab with pistachios). *Balıkpazarı, Gümüşyüzük Sok. 7, Samatya, tel. 212/585–1189 or 212/529–0833. AE, MC, V.*

$$$ **GELIK.** In a two-story 19th-century villa, this restaurant is usually packed with people savoring its delicious specialty: all types of meat roasted in deep cooking wells to produce rich, unusual stews. *Sahilyolu 68–70, tel. 212/560–7284. AE, DC, MC, V.*

$$$ **SARNIÇ.** It's not often you get to dine deep down in an old Roman cistern. Candlelight reflects off the arched yellow-brick walls, and a large fireplace provides warmth in chilly weather. The service is fairly formal, and the fare is a mix of Turkish and Continental, ranging from duck à l'orange to *döner kebap* (meat roasted on a spit). *Sogukçesme Sok., Sultanahmet, tel. 212/512–4291. AE, MC, V.*

$$ **BEYTI.** One of the oldest and most famous meat restaurants in ★ the city, Beyti has grown over the last 55 years from a couple of chairs and a table to a 500-person capacity at its current location near the airport. The restaurant is spread over a terrace and a dozen ornately decorated rooms ensuring that Beyti has never lost its sense of intimacy. Photographs of famous, and sometimes infamous, former guests line the walls of the entrance. Although the starters and main courses are of an invariably high standard, the restaurant is most famous for the dish to which it gave its name,

istanbul dining

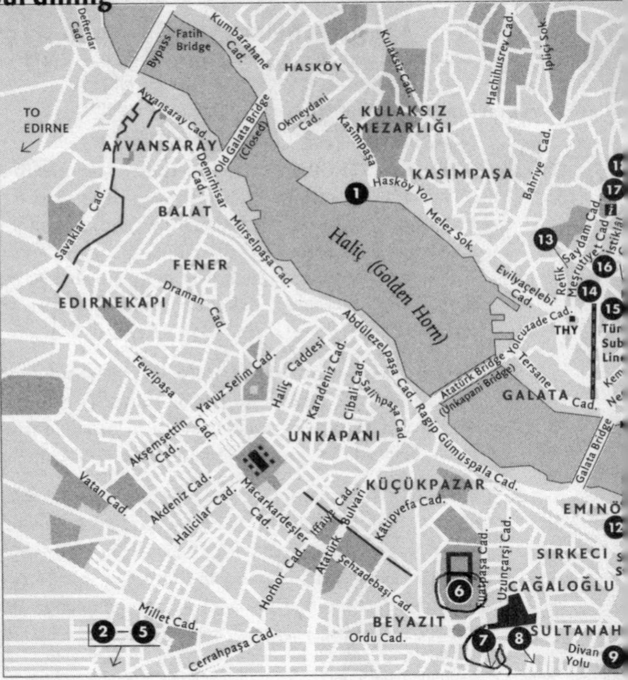

A la Turka, 34
Ayapaşa Russian Restaurant, 29
Beyti, 5
Borsa Lokantasi, 12
Café du Levant, 1
Çatı, 16
Darµlziyafe, 6
Develi Restaurant, 3
Divan, 30
Dört Mevsim, 15
Doy-Doy, 8
Dünya, 33
Fırat, 7
Gelik, 4
Hacı Abdullah, 21
Hacı Salih, 25
Hacıbaba, 23
Hala Manti, 22
Hanedan, 38
Home Store, 32
Iskele, 36
İmroz, 20
Kaşibeyaz, 2
Körfez, 39
Nature and Peace, 24
Mezzaluna, 35
Osmancık, 13
Parsifal, 26
Rejans, 18

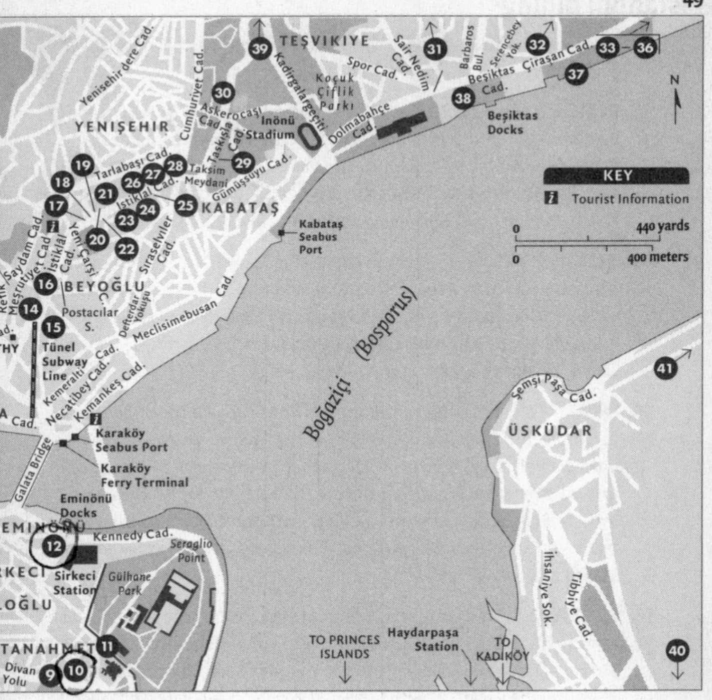

Reşat Paşa Konağı, **40**

Rumeli Café, **9**

Şarabi, **17**

Sarniç, **11**

Le Select, **31**

Sütiş, **28**

Tarihi Sultanahmet Köftecisi, **10**

Tuğra, **37**

Yakup 2, **14**

Zencefil, **27**

Zindan, **19**

spicy meatballs wrapped in thin pastry—*beyti kebabı*. *Orman Sokak 8, Florya, tel. 212/663–2992. MC, V. Closed Mon.*

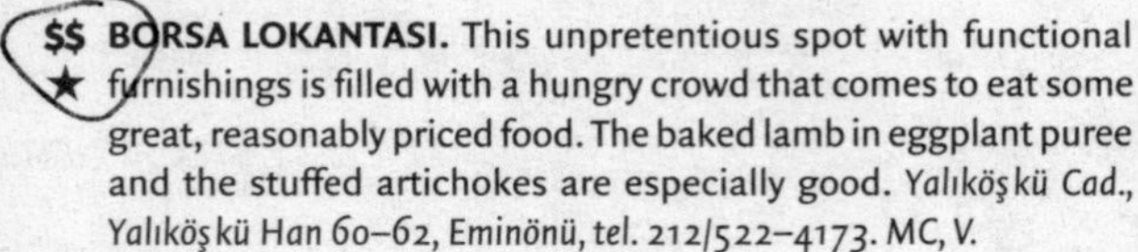

$$ ★ **BORSA LOKANTASI.** This unpretentious spot with functional furnishings is filled with a hungry crowd that comes to eat some great, reasonably priced food. The baked lamb in eggplant puree and the stuffed artichokes are especially good. *Yalıköşkü Cad., Yalıköşkü Han 60–62, Eminönü, tel. 212/522–4173. MC, V.*

$$ ★ **DARULZIYAFE.** This eatery in the Süleymaniye Mosque complex was opened to preserve Ottoman cuisine. House specialties include Süleymaniye soup and Teşrifettin Naim Efendi stew. There is live classical Ottoman *fasıl* music on Saturday evening. *Şifahane Cad. 6, Süleymaniye, tel. 212/511–8414. MC, V.*

$$ **FIRAT.** At this hopping Kumkapı fish house, you barely have time to settle in before food starts coming at you: salads, a savory baked liver dish, shrimp with garlic. In addition to the usual grilled presentations, fish here is baked in a light cream- or tomato-based sauce to great effect. Just point at what you want, but try to save room for dessert. *Çakmaktaş Sok. 11, Kumkapı, tel. 212/517–2308. AE, MC, V.*

$$ ★ **KAŞIBEYAZ.** This large meat restaurant close to the airport was among the first in Istanbul to introduce spicy dishes from eastern Turkey. The house specialty is the pistachio kebab *fıstıklı kebabı*, although the eggplant with browned ground beef (*patlıcanlı kebabı*) and meat patties on eggplant with garlic yogurt and parsley (*alenazik*) are also excellent. *Çatal Sokak 10, Florya, tel. 212/633–2890. Reservations essential on weekends. MC, V.*

$ **DOY-DOY.** *Doy-doy* is a Turkish expression for "full," and you can indeed fill up here for a reasonable sum. Kebabs, *pide* (Turkish pizza), and mezes are served. If you're a vegetarian, the meatless pizzas and salad are good options. Service is friendly, and the menu's prices are ambiguous (sometimes a problem in Istanbul). *Şifa Hamamı Sok. 13, Sultanahmet, tel. 212/517–1588. No credit cards.*

$$ ★ RUMELI CAFÉ RESTAURANT. This little eatery in the heart of the main tourist area offers good food at reasonable prices, including a range of salads and meat dishes. In summer you can sit outside at tables on the sidewalk. *Ticarethane Cad. 8, Sultanahmet, tel. 212/512–0008. No credit cards.*

$ TARIHI SULTANAHMET KÖFTECISI. Although a number of branches exist across the city, this one is the original home of Sultanahmet *köfte* (meatballs). This restaurant has built a small empire from a combination of bare, almost austere decor and an even simpler menu, which has remained virtually unchanged for more than 75 years—meatballs, *piyaz* (boiled white beans in olive oil), and salad. Its location, a couple of minutes' walk from the Blue Mosque and Aya Sofya, makes it ideal for a quick lunch. *Divan Yolu 12, Sultanahmet, tel. 212/513–1438. No credit cards.*

BEYOĞLU AREA

$$ ÇATI. This restaurant on a side street serves hot and cold Turkish dishes and a good buffet. It's on the seventh floor, which allows you to appreciate the architectural splendors of İstiklal Caddesi. Before perusing the menu, ask the waiter about the day's specials. It's open late, and live music is often performed in the evening. *Orhan Apaydın Sok. 20/7, İstiklal Cad., Beyoğlu, tel. 212/251–0000. AE, MC, V. Closed Sun.*

$$ ★ DÖRT MEVSIM (Four Seasons). A handsome Victorian building on the new town's main drag houses this restaurant, noted for its blend of Turkish and French cuisine. It was opened in 1965 by an Anglo-Turkish couple, Gay and Musa, and you'll still find them in the kitchen overseeing the preparation of such delights as shrimp in cognac sauce and baked marinated lamb. *İstiklal Cad. 509, Beyoğlu, tel. 212/293–3941 or 212/243–6320. AE, DC, MC, V. Closed Sun.*

$$ İMROZ. One of the few remaining Greek tavernas in Istanbul, albeit with a Turkish menu, the İmroz is tucked away in a side street, serving meat and fresh fish as well as a range of appetizers, including the spicy cured-meat pastry *pastırmalı böreği*, and the fried cheese dish called *kaşarlı pane*. In summer, all the local restaurants have tables outside, which gives the street an almost carnival atmosphere. *Nevizade Sokak 24, Beyoğlu, tel. 212/249–9073. No credit cards.*

$$ OSMANCIK. On the 23rd floor of the Mercure Hotel, this Turkish restaurant has a 360-degree view of the Bosporus, the Golden Horn, and the rest of Istanbul. The fixed-price menu includes appetizers such as *osmancık boreği* (cheese-filled pastries topped with a yogurt sauce) and grills and all the domestic liquors you want to drink. Entertainment, which starts after 9 PM, comes in the form of traditional Turkish music, followed by a belly dancer. *Meşrutiyet Cad., Tepebası, tel. 212/251–5074. AE, DC, MC, V.*

$$ PARSIFAL. Despite a preponderance of vegetarian dishes, as a concession to carnivores the menu also offers chicken. Small and intimate, with homely hardwood furniture, the Parsifal serves specialties that include quiche, fried soybean patties, and banana crepes. *Kurabiye Sokak 13, İstiklal Cad., Beyoğlu, tel. 212/245–2588. MC, V.*

$$ REJANS. Established by Russian émigrés who fled the Bolshevik revolution, the restaurant is now run by their widows. In the 1930s and 1940s it was one of Istanbul's premiere restaurants. Plaques on the wall bear witness to the famous and infamous who once dined here, from statesmen to World War II spies and diplomats. The decor has remained basically unchanged since the restaurant's heyday, and live Russian music from an accordion-led trio is performed on the balcony Thursday–Saturday. The excellent range of appetizers includes piroshki and borscht, and main courses highlight beef Stroganoff, chicken Kiev, and pork chops. *Emir Nevrut Sok. 17, İstiklal Cad., Beyoğlu, tel. 212/244–1610. Reservations essential Fri.–Sat. MC, V. Closed Sun.*

$$ ŞARABI. This three-story eatery has become famous for offering the largest range of Turkish wines in Istanbul. But it also serves high-quality Mediterranean food, such as steaks, salads and pasta dishes, all at very reasonable prices. *İstiklal Cad. 174, Beyoğlu, tel. 212/244–4609. AE, MC, V.*

$$ ZINDAN. Two hundred years ago this Ottoman *meyhane* was a prison. Today it is a popular haunt of Turkish intellectuals and businesspeople, drawn by superb Turkish cuisine and the atmosphere, created by live *fasıl* (Turkish classical music). *İstiklal Cad., Olivai Han Geçidi 13, Galatasaray, tel. 212/252–7340. No credit cards.*

$ HACI ABDULLAH. Authentic, inexpensive traditional Ottoman and Turkish cuisine has made this a favorite for locals wishing to enjoy good food in a relaxed atmosphere. The restaurant is famous for its appetizers, grilled meats, and seemingly inexhaustible range of pickles and homemade fruit compotes. *Ağa Camii Sakızağacı Cad. 17, Beyoğlu, tel. 212/293–8561. AE, MC, V.*

$ HACIBABA. The menu at this large, cheerful place runs the gamut of Turkish specialties; the lamb kebabs are good, and there are so many mezes that you may never get around to ordering main courses. The shady terrace overlooks a Greek Orthodox churchyard. *İstiklal Cad. 49, Taksim, tel. 212/244–1886 or 212/245–4377. AE, MC, V.*

$ ★ HACI SALIH. You may have to line up for lunch at this tiny, family-run restaurant—it has only 10 tables. But the traditional Turkish fare is worth the wait. Lamb and vegetable dishes are specialties, and though alcohol is not served, you are welcome to bring your own. *Anadolu Han 201/1–2, off Alyon Sok. (off İstiklal Cad.), tel. 212/243–4528. MC, V. Closed Sun. No dinner.*

$ ★ HALA MANTI. As its name suggests, this eatery on busy İstiklal Caddesi specializes in *mantı*, Turkish ravioli. But it also serves excellent *gözleme*, which are thin pastry shells filled with such ingredients as cheese and spinach and then cooked on huge hot plates as you watch. *İstiklal Cad. 211, Beyoğlu, tel. 212/292–7004. No credit cards.*

$ **NATURE AND PEACE.** One of the increasing number of health food restaurants opening in Istanbul, this small eatery serves a range of vegetarian and healthy dishes in a nostalgic, turn-of-the-century atmosphere. *Büyükparmakkapı Sokak 21, Beyoğlu, tel. 212/252–8609. MC, V.*

$ **YAKUP 2.** This cheery hole-in-the-wall is smoky and filled with locals rather than tourists. It can get loud, especially if there is a soccer match on the television. From the stuffed peppers to the octopus salad, the mezes are several notches above average. *Asmalı Mescit Cad. 35–37, tel. 212/249–2925. AE, V.*

$ **ZENCEFIL.** The menu at this pioneering vegetarian restaurant, one of the first to open in Istanbul, changes daily. But it usually includes the house specialty, mushrooms with potatoes, as well as excellent homemade breads and salads. The atmosphere is intimate and cafélike. *Kurabiye Sok. 3, Beyoğlu, tel. 212/244–4082. No credit cards. Closed Sun.*

HASKÖY

$$$$ **CAFÉ DU LEVANT.** Black-and-white floor tiles and turn-of-the-century European furnishings give this café next to the Rahmi Koç Industrial Museum the feel of a Paris bistro. Chefs Giles and Cyril make superb French cuisine, including fillet of turbot with zucchini and tomatoes. For dessert try the crème brûlée or the orange cake with ice cream. *27 Hasköy Cad., Hasköy, tel. 212/235–6328. Reservations essential. AE, DC, MC, V. Closed Mon.*

TAKSIM SQUARE AREA

$$$ **DIVAN.** The Divan, in the hotel of the same name, provides an exception to the unwritten rule that you should avoid hotel restaurants. The menu is a thoughtful blend of Turkish and French

cuisine, the surroundings are elegant, and the service is excellent. *In Divan Hotel, Cumhuriyet Cad. 2, Beyoğlu, tel. 212/231–4100. AE, DC, MC. Closed Sun.*

$$ AYASPAŞA RUSSIAN RESTAURANT. Once run by Russians and now by Turks, the menu and ambience at this restaurant leave little doubt as to its origins. Tapes of Russian folk songs play in the background, and borscht, lemon vodka, and chicken Kiev are served. The beef Stroganoff is also excellent, as are the consistently tasty pork chops. *İnönü Cad. 77/A, Gümüşuyu, Taksim, tel. 212/243–4892. MC, V.*

$$ MEZZALUNA. This place arguably serves the best Italian cuisine in the city. Set in one of Istanbul's most chic neighborhoods, this is a favorite quick lunch venue for those working in the nearby offices. House specialties include linguine, seafood pappardelie and spaghetti vongole. *Abdi İpekçi Caddesi 38/1, Nişantaşı, tel. 212/231–3142. Reservations essential for dinner. AE, MC, V.*

$ SÜTIŞ. This unpretentious spot on the edge of Taksim Square never seems to close. Its cramped frontage opens into a spacious two-tiered interior where the clientele changes with the hours, from office workers eating cheese- or ground-beef-filled börek before work to shoppers and students chatting over tea or a light lunch to bleary-eyed, late-night revelers enjoying Turkish coffee and milk pudding before beginning the journey home. *Sıraselviler Cad. 9/4, Taksim, tel. 212/252–9204. No credit cards.*

ETILER

$$$ HOME STORE. On the ground floor of the Akmerkez shopping mall, in the shop of the same name, Home Store doubles as a bar for the Turkish yuppies spilling out of the offices in the surrounding business district. But the food—whether you come for lunch or an early dinner (it closes at 10 PM)—is very good. The menu includes a range of salads, meat and vegetable dishes, superb soups, and desserts. *Home Store, Akmerkez, Etiler, tel. 212/282–0253. MC, V.*

BOSPORUS

$$$$ **KÖRFEZ.** Call ahead and this restaurant in the picturesque Asian village of Kanlıca can arrange to have you ferried across the Bosporus from Rumeli Hisar. The look is nautical, and the seafood fresh and superbly cooked to order; sample such dishes as flying-fish chowder and sea bass cooked in salt. *Körfez Cad. 78, Kanlıca, tel. 216/413–4314. Reservations essential. AE, DC, MC, V. Closed Mon.*

$$$$ **TUĞRA.** In the Çırağan Palace, this spacious and luxurious restaurant serves the most delectable of long-lost and savored Ottoman recipes, including stuffed bluefish and Circassian chicken. Cookbooks from the Ottoman palace were used to re-create some of the dishes. But that's not all: The Bosporus view is flanked by the palace's marble columns, and ornate glass chandeliers hover above, making you feel like royalty. *Çırağan Cad. 84, tel. 212/258–3377. Reservations essential. Jacket required. AE, DC, MC, V. No lunch.*

$$$$ **LE SELECT.** In an elegant villa in the upmarket Levent neighborhood, Le Select lives up to its name by offering a sumptuous selection ofTurkish, French, and Russian cuisine. House specialties include marinated salmon, sea bass with thyme, and steak in wine sauce. *Manolya Sokak 21, Levent, tel. 212/268–2120. Reservations essential. AE, MC, V.*

$$$ **İSKELE.** Situated on a restored quay on the Bosporus, İskele's romantic setting is more than matched by a fine range of seafood. Ask the waiter for a recommendation for what is in season. Phone ahead for a table by the window or outside on the terrace in warmer weather. *Yahya Kemal Caddesi 1, Rumelihisarı, tel. 212/263–2997. Reservations essential. AE, MC, V.*

$$ **A LA TURKA.** This cozy little restaurant in the Bohemian quarter of Ortaköy serves excellent *mantı* (Turkish ravioli), *gözleme* (meat-, cheese-, or spinach-stuffed phyllo pastry), köfte, and a large range of salads, but no alcohol. In summer outdoor seating is available. *Hazine Sok. 8, Ortaköy, tel. 212/258–7924. MC, V.*

$$ DÜNYA. Right on the Bosporus in bustling Ortaköy, this restaurant has a view of the Bosporus Bridge, the Ortaköy Mosque, and many a passing boat. But as wonderful as these sights are, the food, such as fresh and delicious appetizers of eggplant or octopus salad, is even better. Ask for a table on the terrace as close to the water as possible. *Salhane Sok. 10, Ortaköy, tel. 212/258–6385. MC, V.*

$$ HANEDAN. The emphasis here is on kebabs—all kinds, all of them excellent. The mezes—tabbouleh, hummus, and the flaky pastries known as *böreks*—are tastier than elsewhere. Crisp white linens set off the cool, dark decor. Tables by the front windows offer the advantage of a view of the lively Beşiktaş Ferry terminal. *Çiğdem Sok. 27, Beşiktaş, tel. 212/260–4854. AE, MC, V.*

In This Chapter

Updated by Gareth Jenkins

shopping

IT'S ALMOST IMPOSSIBLE TO LEAVE ISTANBUL without buying something. Whether you're looking for trinkets and souvenirs, kilims and carpets, brass and silverware, leather, old books, prints and maps, or furnishings and clothes (Turkish textiles are among the best in the world), you can find them in Istanbul. Shopping in the city also provides a snapshot of its contrasts and contradictions, from migrants from eastern Turkey selling their wares on the streets to the leisurely, time-honored haggling in bazaars and back alleys to the credit cards and bar codes of the plush, upscale Western-style department stores.

The bazaars, all brimming with copper and brassware, hand-painted ceramics, carved alabaster and onyx, fabrics, richly colored carpets, and (truth be told) tons of tourist junk, are the main places to shop in Turkey. You won't roam the bazaars too long before someone tries to lure you in with a free glass of *çay* (tea), whether you're a serious shopper or are just browsing.

Antiques

Beware of antiques. When dealing with pieces purported to be more than 100 years old, chances are you will end up with an expensive fake, which is just as well since it's illegal to export the real thing without a government permit (and they are very strict about this). If what you covet is less than 100 years old, snap it up. If your purchase looks old, it is advisable to have its date authenticated by a local museum to avoid problems when you leave the country.

Note, too, that Turkish antiquities law applies to every piece of detritus, so don't pick up anything off the ground at archaeological sites. You may be offered *eski para* (old money) and other "antiquities"; these are all fake, and if they were not, they couldn't be taken out of the country. You are much better off buying high-quality copies from museum gift shops rather than from peddlers at archaeological sites.

Rugs

Persistent salesmen and affordable prices make it hard to leave Turkey without flat-woven kilims or other rugs. No matter what you've planned, sooner or later you'll end up in the cool of a carpet shop listening to a sales rap. Regardless of how many cups of tea you drink and how persistent the salesmen may be, do not let yourself be pressured into making a purchase you do not want. Salesmen will insist they can't lower the price, but they almost always do.

If you buy a rug or kilim and can manage to take it home on the plane, do that. If you have purchased a number of rugs, you might consider shipping them yourself (or letting the store do it for you if it has a good reputation). Note, however, that you are taking a risk by shipping your rug and that it will probably take a while to get to you.

Other Local Specialties

Made of a light, porous stone found only in Turkey, meerschaum pipes are prized for their cool smoke; look for a centered hole and even walls. You can also buy tiles and porcelain, though modern work doesn't compare with older craftsmanship. Some spices, saffron foremost among them, can be purchased for a fraction of their cost back home. Another good deal is jewelry, because you pay by weight and not for design—but watch out for tin and alloys masquerading as silver. Turkey is also known for its leather goods, but it's better to stick with merchandise off the rack and steer clear of made-to-order goods.

Bargaining

Outside the bazaars, prices are often fixed, though in resort areas many shopkeepers will bargain if you ask for a better price. But in bazaars the operative word is "bargain." As much social ritual as a battle of wills, it can be great fun once you get the hang of it.

There is no rule of thumb for the difference between the first price you are offered and how much the seller will eventually accept. If you are sure of how much the article is worth, or how much you are prepared to pay, then make an offer 15% to 25% under it. If not, don't state a figure, even if the seller asks you for one. Just smile, shake your head sadly, and say the price he is asking is too expensive. He will invariably lower it. Express regret that it is still expensive and ask for the final price. The figure you are then given won't, of course, be the real final price. But the speed and amount by which the seller changes his supposed "final price" will give you an idea of how close you are to the lowest he will go—and where to pitch your counteroffer.

Don't forget that you can always tell the seller that, as much as you appreciate his time and admire the quality of the item in question, it is still too expensive, and then get up to leave. The lowest price invariably comes when the seller thinks he is about to lose a customer; and you can always double back into the store. Note, however, that it's both bad manners and bad business to bargain aggressively or to decline to buy once the seller has accepted your offer.

MARKETS

The **Grand Bazaar** (☞ Grand Bazaar to Eminönü in Here and There) is a neighborhood unto itself and a trove of all things

Turkish—carpets, brass, copper, jewelry, textiles, and leather goods. The fashions are not bad either—though not quite up to Italian style, they're dramatically less expensive. **Nuruosmaniye Caddesi,** one of the major streets leading to the Grand Bazaar, is lined with some of Istanbul's most stylish shops, with an emphasis on fine carpets, jewelry, and made-in-Turkey fashions.

A flea market is held in **Beyazıt Square,** near the Grand Bazaar, every Sunday. In recent years it has become a favorite with street traders from the former Eastern Bloc, who sell everything from cheap vodka and electronic goods to cast-off Red Army uniforms. The **Arasta Bazaar,** in Sultanahmet, is one of few markets open on Sunday; you can get a lot of the same items here as at the Grand Bazaar, and the atmosphere is a lot calmer.

Definitely worth seeing is the **Egyptian Bazaar,** also known as the Spice Market. The **Balıkpazarı** (Fish Market) sells, despite its name, everything connected with food, from picnic supplies to exotic spices and teas; it's on Beyoğlu Caddesi off İstiklal Caddesi. **Sahaflar Çarşışı** is home to a bustling book market, with old and new editions; most are in Turkish, but English and other languages are represented. The market is open daily, though Sunday has the most vendors. Along the Bosporus in the **Ortaköy** neighborhood is a Sunday crafts market with street entertainment.

SHOPPING AREAS

İstiklal Caddesi is a street with everything from stores selling old books and Levis to the Vakko department store to a less stylish Turkish version of Saks Fifth Avenue. The **high-fashion district** centers on Halâskârgazi Caddesi and Rumeli Caddesi in Nişantaşı, 1 km (½ mi) north of İstiklal Caddesi. Here you will find the best efforts of Turkish fashion designers.

Bağdat Caddesi, Bahariye Caddesi, and the **Carrefoursa** mall, all on the Asian side, are the places to find more suburban shopping venues. The **Galleria** mall, in Ataköy near the airport, has more than 100 stores selling foreign and local brand-name clothing. **Akmerkez,** in the Etiler district, is a large and luxurious mall whose stores stock recognized trademarks. The center has a movie theater, a restaurant, a fast-food court, and cafés.

SPECIALTY STORES

Antiques

Sofa (Nuruosmaniye Cad. 42) stocks a fascinating collection of old maps and prints, original İznik and Kütahya ceramics, vintage jewelry, and assorted other treasures. **Çığır Kitabevi** (Sahaflar Çarşışı 17) has an impressive collection of old books, many of them illustrated. **Ory & Ady** (Serifagu Sok. 7–8, in the bedestan section of the Grand Bazaar) specializes in Ottoman miniatures, illustrations, and prints.

If you know old books, you can pick up bargains from the dozen or so shops at the **Kasımpaşa** flea market (Kulaksız Cad. 5, Büyük Çarşı, Kasımpaşa); the **Horhor** flea market, in Aksaray (Kırık Tulumba Sok. 13–22, Aksaray); or, on the Asian side of the city, the **Kadıköy** flea market (Çakıroğlu İşhanı, Tellalzade Sok., Moda Cad., Kadıköy).

Carpets and Kilims

You can find carpet shops at nearly every turn, all stocking rugs for a variety of prices. Each shop has slightly different pieces, so it's best to look at several to get a feel for the market. On the other hand, there's nothing wrong with buying from the first shop you go into if you find something you love.

Some of the better shops in Istanbul include: **Adnan Hassan** (Halıcılar Cad. 90); **Al-Dor** (Faruk Ayanoğlu Cad. 5–8); **Celletin Senghor** (Grand Bazaar); and **Ensar** (Arasta Bazaar 109). Also try the shops along Nuruosmaniye Caddesi, particularly **Çınar,** at No. 6.

Clothing

Angel Leather (Nuruosmaniye Cad. 67) has kidskin suede and leather skirts and jackets; the best of Turkish leather is on a par with Italian leather quality wise, though the designs are not as stylish. Fashionable **Beymen** (Halâskârgazi Cad. 230) is Istanbul's version of Bloomingdale's. **Beymen Club** (Rumeli Cad. 81 and Akmerkez shopping mall, in Etiler) sells casual Polo-style clothing. **Silk and Cashmere** (Akmerkez shopping mall, in Etiler, or Galleria shopping mall, in Ataköy, or on the Asian side, the Carrefour shopping mall, in Kozyatağı) carries a fine selection of high-quality, affordable silk and cashmere menswear and women's wear.

Sube (Arasta Bazaar 131) has handmade kilim slippers with leather soles and kilim boots for a fraction of their prices in the United States. **Vakko** (İstiklal Cad. 123–125, Beyoğlu or Akmerkez shopping mall, in Etiler, or on the Asian side, Bağdat Cad. 422, in Suadiye) is one of Turkey's oldest and most elegant fashion houses, with an excellent fabric department. Former president Bill Clinton could occasionally be seen sporting one of the Vakko ties presented to him by visiting Turkish delegates. Turkish designer **Zeki Triko** (Valikonağı Cad.) sells his own bathing suits, completely up-to-date, at his eponymous boutiques.

English-Language Bookstores

Many larger hotels and souvenir shops in the old city stock some English-language newspapers and books, mostly guides to the more famous sights. Although it is sometimes possible to find U.S. daily newspapers, most cost $10 or more. A more comprehensive range can be found at specialty stores in Beyoğlu and the fashionable shopping districts of Nişantaşı and Levent. Books originally published outside Turkey are marked up 15%–75%.

Some of the larger bookstores carrying English-language books include: **Homer** (Yeni Çarşı Cad. 28A, Galatasaray, Beyoğlu, tel.

212/249–5902); **Galeri Kayseri** (Divanyolu 58, Sultanahmet 34410, tel. 212/512–0456); **Pandora** (Büyük Parmakkapı Sok. 3, Beyoğlu, tel. 212/243–3503); **Remzi Kitabevi** (Akmerkez shopping mall, basement floor, No. 121, Levent, tel. 212/282–0245; Rumeli Cad. 44, Nişantaşı, tel. 212/234–5475); and **Robinson Crusoe** (İstiklal Cad. 389, Tünel, Beyoğlu, tel. 212/293–6968).

A number of stores specialize in secondhand books, many in English, from dog-eared thrillers to rare old texts about the city. These include: **Aslıhan Sahaflar Çarsısı** (Galatasaray Balık Pazarı, Beyoğlu); **Librairie de Pera** (Galip Dede Sok. 22, Tünel, tel. 212/245–4998); and a cluster of antiquarian booksellers in the **Sahaflar Çarsısı** (Sahaflar Çarsı Sok., Beyazıt).

Jewelry

The most common type of jewelry you'll see are amber necklaces and ethnic Turkish silver jewelry threaded with coral and lapis lazuli. **Georges Basoğlu** (Cevahir Bedestan 36–37) and **Venus** (Kalpakcılar Cad. 160) sell distinctive and original pieces. **Nasit** (Arasta Bazaar 111) often carries vintage silver jewelry as well as new items. **Urart** (Abdi İpekçi Cad. 181) has chic interpretations of ancient Anatolian designs.

In This Chapter

Updated by Gareth Jenkins

outdoor activities and sports

WANDERING THROUGH THE CITY ITSELF is probably your best bet for exercise. However, you can also take a dip at an area beach, catch an odd game of golf or jog in one of Istanbul's many parks. If you want to be a spectator, soccer is a citywide obsession.

PARTICIPANT SPORTS

BEACHES

Even though local boys playfully dive into the sea even in the heart of the city, swimming is not recommended. The European shore of the Sea of Marmara is muddy and unpleasant, the Bosporus is famous for its dangerously strong currents, and either way, the water is pretty cold and heavily polluted. Stick with the hotel pool. If you must, your best bet is to make the hour-long drive to the area's nicest beach, at **Kilyos** on the Black Sea. Avoid the municipal beaches at Florya, a suburb on the European side, where bacteria have dangerously contaminated the waters.

GOLF

Istanbul is not a noted golfing destination; you won't find Sawgrass or Pebble Beach, but the courses are perfectly fine if you need a fix. Itinerant players are welcomed at the **Istanbul**

Distance Conversion Chart

Kilometers/Miles

To change kilometers (km) to miles (mi), multiply km by .621. To change mi to km, multiply mi by 1.61.

km to mi	mi to km
1 = .62	1 = 1.6
2 = 1.2	2 = 3.2
3 = 1.9	3 = 4.8
4 = 2.5	4 = 6.4
5 = 3.1	5 = 8.1
6 = 3.7	6 = 9.7
7 = 4.3	7 = 11.3
8 = 5.0	8 = 12.9

Meters/Feet

To change meters (m) to feet (ft), multiply m by 3.28. To change ft to m, multiply ft by .305.

m to ft	ft to m
1 = 3.3	1 = .30
2 = 6.6	2 = .61
3 = 9.8	3 = .92
4 = 13.1	4 = 1.2
5 = 16.4	5 = 1.5
6 = 19.7	6 = 1.8
7 = 23.0	7 = 2.1
8 = 26.2	8 = 2.4

Golf Club (Büyükdere Cad., Ayazağa, tel. 212/264–0742). The **Kemer Golf & Country Club** (Kemerburgaz in the Belgrade Forest, 25 mins from Istanbul, tel. 212/239–7913) has a nine-hole course. A little farther afield, the **Klassis Country and Golf Clubb** (Kemer Köyü, 45 mins from Istanbul, tel. 212/748–4600) has a good standard 18-hole, par 72 course and often hosts international tournaments.

JOGGING AND WALKING

If exploring the city's streets still leaves you wanting more exercise, try one of its parks. The wooded slopes of **Yıldız Park,** just north of the Çirağan Palace, are usually blissfully uncrowded. **Belgrade Forest** has enticing wooded paths and a 6.5-km (4-mi) walking and jogging track around the shores of old reservoirs. **Emirgân Park** is noted for its flower gardens and Bosporus views. **Gülhane Park** is conveniently located, right alongside Topkapı Palace.

SPECTATOR SPORTS

SOCCER

Soccer is Turkey's passion, and **Turkish Division One** is the country's major league. Matches take place from September through May at İnönü Stadium, Fenerbahçe Stadium, and Ali Sami Yen Stadium. You can get tickets at the stadiums or ask at your hotel for help. If you prefer comfort to atmosphere, ask someone at your hotel—almost everyone is a passionate fan of one of the city's teams—for the schedule of televised games.

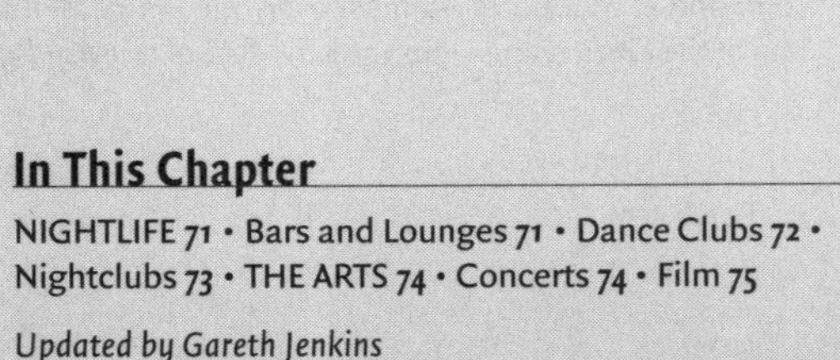

In This Chapter

Updated by Gareth Jenkins

nightlife and the arts

ISTANBUL'S ARTS AND ENTERTAINMENT OFFERINGS run the gamut from jazz dens to belly dancing. For upcoming events, reviews, and other information, pick up a copy of *The Guide*, a reliable bimonthly English-language publication that has listings of hotels, bars, restaurants, and events, as well as features about Istanbul. The English-language *Turkish Daily News* is another good resource both for listings and for keeping abreast of what is happening in Turkish and international politics.

NIGHTLIFE

Bars and Lounges

With views of the Bosporus and a top-notch restaurant next door, **Bebek Bar** (Bebek Ambassadeurs Hotel, Cevdet Paşa Cad. 113, Bebek, tel. 212/263–3000) attracts a dressed-up crowd. **Beyoğlu Pub** (İstiklal Cad. 140/17, Beyoğlu, tel. 212/252–3842), in a pleasant garden in summer and indoors in winter, draws moviegoers from nearby theaters and expatriates.

At the opposite end of İstiklal Caddesi from Taksim Square, **Café Gramofon** (Tünel Meyd. 3, Tünel, tel. 212/293–0786), a café during the day, becomes a jazz bar evenings Tuesday–Saturday. The latest music and spicy Asian food have made **Buddha Bar** (Kuruçeşme Caddesi 22–24, Etiler, tel. 212/265–9016) a firm favorite with the Istanbul jet set.

Hayal Kahvesi (Büyükparmakkapı Sok. 19, Beyoğlu, tel. 212/224–2558) is a smoky, crowded late-night hangout for a mostly

young crowd that likes live (and loud) rock and blues. **Harry's Jazz Bar** (Hyatt Regency Hotel, Takışla, Taksim, tel. 212/225–7000) is a popular hangout for foreign and Turkish professionals, drawn by its avant-garde decor, its live music, which is often blues or rock rather than jazz, and its potent cocktails.

The Irish pub **James Joyce** (Zambak Sokak 6, İstiklal Cad., Beyoğlu, tel. 212/244–0241) offers a wide selection of imported beers and spirits, including the Irish staple, Guinness, and a fine range of malt whiskeys. There is live music every night and Irish music on weekends.

The **Orient Express Bar** (Pera Palace Hotel, Meşrutiyet Cad. 98, tel. 212/251–4560) is hard to beat for its turn-of-the-century atmosphere; you can't help but sense the ghosts of the various kings, queens, and Hollywood stars who have passed through its doors.

Roxy (Arslanyatağı Sok. 9, Sıraselviler, Taksim, tel. 212/245–6539) is a popular bar with a spirited, young crowd and live music; it also serves a good range of foods to snack on between drinks and music.

If you are looking to sample the latest in Turkish music, then **Kehribar** (Divan Hotel, Cumhuriyet Cad. 2, Taksim, tel. 212/231–4100) has live pop and jazz. Zihni, which is only open in summer, is on a terrace on the shore of the Bosporus, with idyllic views; it can become crowded on weekends (Muallim Naci Cad. 19, Ortaköy, tel. 212/258–1154).

Dance Clubs

Dance clubs get rolling by about 10 and usually keep going until 3 or 4 in the morning. **Club 14** (Abdülhakhamit Cad. 63, Talimhane, tel. 212/256–2121) is, as its hours—11 PM–4 AM—suggest, a lively late-night spot. The classy **Club 29** (Paşabahçe Yolu, Çubuklu, tel. 216/322–2829) holds forth in a faux-Roman villa by the Bosporus on the Asian side from mid-June through September.

Havana (Fargo İş Merkezi, Büyükdere Cad., Esentepe, tel. 212/213–0136) is the place to be seen for young socialites. It opens at 7 for dinner, but the dancing really gets going after 10. In the summer it relocates to Muallim Naci Caddesi, in Ortaköy, (tel. 212/259–5919), where it has become the city's leading open-air dance spot. **Switch** (Muammer Karaca Çıkmazı 3, İstiklal Cad., Beyoğlu, tel. 212/292–7458) is Istanbul's newest and most up-to-date underground club, with guest Turkish and foreign DJs on weekends.

Nightclubs

Probably a good deal tamer than you might have expected to find in Istanbul, the city's nightclub shows include everything from folk dancers to jugglers, acrobats, belly dancers, and singers. Some routines are fairly touristy but still fun. Typically, dinner is served after 8, and floor shows start around 10. Be aware that these are not inexpensive once you've totaled up drink, food, and cover. Reservations are a good idea; be sure to specify whether you're coming for dinner as well as the show or just for drinks.

Note that at the seedy striptease places off İstiklal Caddesi, the goal is to get customers to pay outrageous drink prices for questionable companionship. Those unwary enough to enter such places have reported being physically intimidated when questioning a drinks bill that has run into the hundreds of dollars.

Galata Tower (Kuledibi, tel. 212/245–1160) is high atop the new town in a round room sheathed in windows; the ambience is strictly hotel lounge, and the Turkish dishes are only average. The fixed prices are around $70 for the show and dinner and $40 for the show and a drink.

Comfortable, well-established **Kervansaray** (Cumhuriyet Cad. 30, tel. 212/247–1630) hosts a varied floor show, including two belly dancers, regional folk dances, and medleys of songs from around the world; it serves a variety of Turkish dishes and costs about $70 for the show and dinner, $50 for the show and a drink. **Orient House** (Tiyatro Cad. 27, Eminönü, tel. 212/517–6163 or 212/517–3488) presents a floor show with belly dancers and Turkish folk dancing, along with good traditional Turkish food. It's about $75 for the show and dinner and $50 for the show and a drink.

THE ARTS

The **Istanbul International Festival,** held from late June through mid-July, attracts renowned artists performing modern and classical music, ballet, opera, and theater. Shows occur throughout the city in historic buildings, such as Aya Irini and Rumeli Hisar. To order tickets in advance, apply to the Istanbul Foundation for Culture and Arts (Kültür ve Sanat Concer Vakfi, İstiklal Cad. 146, Beyoğlu, 80070, tel. 212/293–3133).

In May, Istanbul hosts an **International Theater Festival,** which attracts major stage talent from eastern and western Europe. Because there is no central ticket agency, ask your hotel to help you get tickets or inquire at the box office or local tourist offices.

Concerts

The **Aksanat Cultural Center** (Akbank Bldg., İstiklal Cad., Beyoğlu, tel. 212/252–3500) shows classical and jazz concerts on a large laser-disc screen, presents films, and hosts exhibitions.

Istanbul's main concert hall is **Atatürk Kültür Merkezi** (tel. 212/251–5600), in Taksim Square. The Istanbul State Symphony performs here from October through May, and ballet and dance companies do shows year-round.

The **Cemal Reşit Rey Concert Hall** (Gümüş Sok., Harbiye, tel. 212/231–5498), close to the Istanbul Hilton, hosts recitals and chamber and symphonic music, modern dance, rock, folk, and jazz concerts performed by international talent. Tickets are often less than half the price they might be in the United States or Europe.

Film

Some theaters on the strip of İstiklal Caddesi between Taksim and Galatasaray show the latest from Hollywood, with a few current European or Turkish movies thrown in. There are also plush, modern theaters at the Istanbul Princess Hotel, in Maslak, and Akmerkez shopping center, in Levent. It's a good idea to purchase tickets in advance for the latter, particularly on weekends.

Most foreign films are shown with their original soundtrack and Turkish subtitles, although many children's films are dubbed into Turkish. Look for the words *Ingilizce* (English) or *orijinal* (original language). Films in languages other than English will have subtitles in Turkish. When in doubt, ask at the ticket office whether the film is dubbed (*dublaj* in Turkish) or subtitled (*altyazılı* in Turkish).

The annual **Istanbul International Film Festival,** which is held in the first two weeks of April, presents films from around the world; ask for a schedule at any box office and make sure to purchase tickets in advance. Seats are reserved.

In This Chapter

Updated by Gareth Jenkins

side trips

IF A FEW DAYS IN ISTANBUL HAS YOUR head spinning, serenity is just a short ferry ride away. A trip to the Princes Islands offers a taste of the simple life with quiet beaches, wooded hills, and carriage rides. If you have time to travel farther, Edirne has all the attractions of Istanbul—Ottomon-style wooden houses, resplendent mosques, authentic bazaars—without the crowds or bustle of the big city.

PRINCES ISLANDS

20 km (12 mi) off the coast of Istanbul from Sultanahmet.

The nine islands in the Sea of Marmara have proven a useful amenity for Istanbul. In the days when the city was known as Constantinople, religious undesirables sought refuge here; in the time of the sultans, the islands provided a convenient place to exile untrustworthy hangers-on.

By the turn of the last century, well-heeled businessmen had staked their claim and built many of the Victorian gingerbread–style houses that lend the islands their charm. But the islands remained a place of refuge. In the 1930s Büyükada, the largest of the islands, was the home for several years of the exiled Leon Trotsky.

Today the islands provide a leafy retreat from Istanbul. Restrictions on development and a ban on automobiles maintain the old-fashioned peace and quiet—transportation is by horse-drawn carriage or bicycle. Though there are no real sights and populations swell significantly on summer weekends, the Princes Islands are perfect for relaxed outings. Of the nine islands, only four have regular ferry service, and only the two largest, Büyükada and Heybeli, are of real interest. Both are hilly and wooded, and the fresh breeze is gently pine scented.

BÜYÜKADA

To the left as you leave the ferry, you will see a handful of restaurants with names like Monte Carlo, Capri, and Milano. They are pleasant dives, though somewhat overpriced, and there's little difference among them. **Yörük Ali Plaj,** the public beach on the west side of the island, is an easy walk from the harbor and also has a little restaurant.

To see the island's splendid old Victorian houses, walk to the clock tower and bear right. Carriages are available at the clock tower square. The carriage tour winds up hilly lanes lined with gardens filled with jasmine, mimosa, and imported palm trees. After all of Istanbul's mosques and palaces, the frilly pastel houses come as something of a surprise. But it's quite easy to imagine men in panama hats and women with parasols having picnics out in the garden.

You can have your buggy driver wait while you make the 20-minute hike up Yücetepe Hill to the **Greek Monastery of St. George,** where there are three chapels and a sacred fountain believed to have healing waters. As you walk up the path, notice the pieces of cloth, string, and paper that visitors have tied to the bushes and trees in hope of a wish coming true. This is a popular Orthodox Christian pilgrimage site, especially at Greek Easter, when hundreds make the hike barefoot. If you're lucky, the outdoor restaurant next to the monastery will be serving its homemade wine.

Eating Out

There is little difference from one spot on Büyükada's restaurant row to the next. The best bet is to look at a menu and ask to see the dishes on display. If a place is crowded with Turks, it is usually good.

Where to Stay

$$$ SPLENDID HOTEL. For character, it's hard to beat this wooden turn-of-the-century hotel, with its old-fashioned furniture, large rooms, and Ottoman Victorian styling. The building is topped by twin white domes, copies of those at the Hotel Negresco in Nice. It's difficult to get a room on summer weekends unless you book ahead. *23 Nisan Cad. 71, Büyükada, 81330, tel. 216/382–6950, fax 216/382–6775. 70 rooms with bath. Restaurant, pool. MC, V. Closed Oct.–Apr.*

HEYBELI

The big building to the left of the dock, the **Deniz Kuvvetler** (Turkish Naval Academy), is open to visitors every day except Sunday, though there's not really that much to see. To the right of Heybeli's dock are teahouses and cafés stretching along the waterfront. You can take a leisurely carriage ride, stopping, if the mood strikes, at one of the island's several small, sandy, and rarely crowded beaches—the best are on the north shore at the foot of **Değirmen Burnu** (Windmill Point) and **Değirmen Tepesi** (Windmill Hill). You can rent a rowboat for a few dollars at these beaches for the trip out to one of the other Princes Islands across the way.

You will also pass the ruined monastery of the **Panaghia,** founded in the 15th century. Though damaged by fires and earthquakes, the chapel and several red-tile-roofed buildings remain. Carriages here do not climb the hills above the harbor, where the old mansions and gardens are. The walk, however, is not that strenuous.

Where to Stay

$$$ MERIT HALKI PALAS. A member of the Merit chain, the Halki Palas was opened in 1994 after its predecessor, which had been built in the 1850s, burned down. But the character of the old hotel has been retained, with white-painted wood, ornate eaves, and large, airy rooms. It's one of the most restful hotels in Istanbul, and though the island has few sights of its own, the old city is only an hour away by ferry. *Refah Şehitleri Cad. 88, 81340, Heybeliada, tel. 216/351–8890, fax 216/351–8483. 45 rooms with bath. Restaurant, pool. MC, V. www.merithotel.com*

PRINCES ISLANDS ESSENTIALS

Arriving and Departing

Ferries (80¢–$1.70) make the trip from Sirkeci or Bostancı (Asian side) docks in half an hour to an hour, depending on where they depart. Go straight to Büyükada and catch a local ferry to Heybeli later. You must pay each way to and from Istanbul but can travel for free between the islands themselves.

For the return journey you can buy a ticket on the islands, but you must hold on to it and hand it over on disembarkation in Istanbul. In summer, the early evening ferries returning to the mainland are often very crowded on weekends. Much quicker, though less romantic, is the sea bus, departing from Kabataş near the Dolmabahçe Mosque and from Bostancı sea-bus terminals on the Asian side. Buy tokens for the sea bus at the terminals.

Getting Around

Since no cars are allowed on the islands, you do most of your exploring on foot. Horse-drawn carriage tours cost $10 to $15. The other, perhaps more strenuous but definitely fun, option, is to rent a bicycle ($2 per hour) from one of the shops near the clock tower on Büyükada. To get from one of the Princes Islands to the other, hop aboard any of several daily ferries.

EDIRNE

235 km (146 mi) northwest of Istanbul.

Unlike Istanbul, which every conqueror and pretender within marching distance hoped to have as his capital, Thrace was the sort of region that most warriors passed on through. The climate is harsh—sizzling in summer, bitter in winter—and the landscape unexceptional. But the area has some worthy sights, particularly Edirne, founded in the 2nd century AD as Hadrianopolis by the Roman emperor Hadrian. The city has been fought over by Bulgars, crusaders, Turks, Greeks, and Russians through the centuries, though once the Ottoman capital was moved to Istanbul, it became something of a picturesque backwater. The overhanging balconies of traditional Ottoman wooden houses shade Edirne's still-cobbled lanes, and its rich collection of mosques and monuments remains mostly unspoiled by the concrete towers so prevalent in Turkey's boomtowns.

Hürriyet Meydanı, Edirne's central square, makes a good starting point. Standing in the middle of it is a monument to the city's great passion, wrestling: Two enormous wrestlers steal the spotlight from the obligatory Atatürk statue.

Just off the north side of the Hürriyet Meydanı (Freedom Square) is the **Üç Şerefeli Cami** (Mosque with Three Galleries), built between 1437 and 1447. The galleries circle the tallest of the four minarets, which are notable for their fine brick inlay. On the mosque grounds is the 15th-century **Sokurlu Hamam,** built by Sinan, and one of the country's more elegant baths. It is open to the public from about 8 AM until 10 PM and costs $4 for a bath, $10 for a bath with massage.

Walking east from the square along Talat Paşa Caddesi brings you to the **Eski Cami** (Old Mosque). The mosque is appropriately named: Completed in 1414, it is the city's oldest. The huge-scale calligraphy illustrating quotes from the Koran and naming the prophets is exceptional in its grace and intricacy.

Adjoining it is the **Rüstempaşa Kervansaray** (Rüstempaşa Caravansary), restored and reopened as a hotel, just as it was in the 16th century. Also alongside the mosque is the 14-domed **bedestan** (market), and one block away, the **Ali Paşa Bazaar.** Both are more authentic than Istanbul's Grand Bazaar, as the wares sold—coffeepots, kilims, soap shaped like fruits and vegetables, towels—are meant for locals rather than tourists. *Talat Paşa Cad., east from Hürriyet Meyd., no phone. Free. Daily 9–7.*

The **Selimiye Cami** (Selimiye Mosque), not Istanbul's Süleymaniye, is the mosque Sinan described as his masterpiece, and it is certainly one of the most beautiful buildings in Turkey. Today a statue of the architect stands in front, but it is hardly necessary; the mosque remains his greatest monument. The architect was 85 years old when it was completed. The central dome, more than 100 ft in diameter and 148 ft high, rests on eight pillars, set into the walls so as not to disturb the interior space. External buttresses help support the weight of 999 windows; legend has it that Sultan Selim thought 1,000 might be a bit greedy. The marble minbar (pulpit) is exquisitely carved, and the mihrab is set back in an apse adorned with exceptional İznik tiles.

The *medrese* (mosque compound) houses Edirne's **Türk-Islâm Eserleri Müzesi** (Museum of Turkish and Islamic Art), which displays Islamic calligraphy and photos of local wrestlers, as well as collections of weapons and jewelry from ancient Thrace, folk costumes, kilims, and fine embroidery. *Hürriyet Meyd. Free. Daily sunrise–sunset; usually closed to tourists at prayer times, particularly Fri. noon prayers.*

The other great mosque in Edirne is the striking **Beyazıt Cami** (Beyazıt Mosque), on the outskirts of the city across the Tunca River. The immense complex is about a 20-minute walk northwest from Hürriyet Meydanı via the fine-hewn, six-arched **Beyazıt Bridge,** which dates from the 1480s, as does the mosque. You can also take a *dolmuş* (shared taxi) from the square.

The mosque was built by the Sultan Beyazıt, hence its name, at the end of the 15th century. The complex includes both the mosque itself—with a remarkable indented dome and a beautifully fretted mihrab—and two schools, a hospital, a kitchen, and storage depots. Apart from visiting tourists or a handful of young boys from the neighboring village playing soccer in the shadow of its walls, the complex is usually deserted by all but the custodian and fluttering pigeons, making it not only one of the most peaceful spots in Edirne but also a poignant reminder of the city's imperial past. *Head northwest from Hürriyet Meydanı, across Beyazıt Bridge, no phone. Free. Daily sunrise–sunset during summer; mosque is often locked during winter, but custodian will sometimes open it up.*

Sarayiçi, a field with an arena on one side, is the site of Edirne's famous wrestling tournament. Usually held in June, it is the best known of those held in villages throughout the country: Its burly, olive-oil-coated men have been facing off annually here for more than 600 years. Thousands of spectators turn out. Sarayiçi is a 20-minute walk up the Tunca River from Benazıt Cami.

EATING OUT

$ BULVAR KEBAP. Just north of the main square on the way to the Selimiye Mosque, the Bulvar offers not only kebabs but a tasty range of *pide*, filled with ground beef, cheese, and grilled lamb served in clean, if unprepossessing, surroundings. *Emekli Öğretmenler Derneği Altı., tel. 284/225–6624. No credit cards.*

$ EMIRGAN. On the outskirts of town amid plane trees on the western bank of the Meriç River, this popular local haunt serves a passable range of Turkish meatballs, *köfte* and *şiş kebab*. In summer you can sit outside and watch the river flow. *Karaağaç Yolu, tel. 284/212–2906. No credit cards.*

WHERE TO STAY

$$ HOTEL RÜSTEM PAŞA KERVANSARAY. Built in the 1500s, reputedly by the celebrated architect Sinan, today this hotel is the most impressive in Edirne, at least from the outside. The inside is more functional: Rooms have high ceilings and decorative fireplaces, plain furniture, and low, single beds; avoid rooms near the nightclub, which are noisy. The building sprawls around a pleasant courtyard full of flowers and shaded by a huge plane tree. *İki Kapılı Han Cad. 57, Sabuni Mah., 22800, tel. 284/225–2195 or 284/225–6119, fax 284/212–0462. 79 rooms with bath. Restaurant, nightclub, bar. MC, V.*

$ ŞABAN AÇIGÖZ OTELI. Modest and nondescript, the Açıgöz Oteli is efficient, clean, and well located, just off the main square and opposite the Kervansaray. The hotel does not have the charm of its neighbor, but its rooms are functional, with all the basic amenities. A small restaurant serves breakfast but no midday or evening meals. *Tahmis Meyd., Çilingirler Cad. 9, 22800, tel. 284/213–1404 or 284/213–0313, fax 284/213–4516. 34 rooms with shower. Restaurant. MC, V.*

EDIRNE ESSENTIALS

Arriving and Departing

Buses headed for Edirne depart frequently from Istanbul's Esenler Terminal. The trip takes four hours and costs $4. If you're going by car, take the toll road—the E80 TEM (the toll from Istanbul to Edirne costs $3.50), which is faster and much easier than Route 100. The trip takes about 2½ hours. Three trains leave Istanbul's Sirkeci Station daily for the painfully slow 6- to 10-hour trip; the cost is about $5, so you are better off taking the bus or driving.

Getting Around

The bus and train stations are on the outskirts of town, too far to walk. Take a taxi into the center, asking for Hürriyet Meydanı. Sights in town can all be reached on foot.

Contacts and Resources

Edirne's **tourist information office** (Talat Paşa Cad., near Hürriyet Meyd., tel. 284/213–9208) is open every day in summer and is generally closed off-season.

In This Chapter

Updated by Gareth Jenkins

where to stay

ALMOST EVERYTHING THAT YOU PROBABLY want to see in Istanbul is in the older part of town, but the big modern hotels are mainly around Taksim Square in the new town and along the Bosporus, a 15- or 20-minute cab ride away. The Aksaray, Laleli, Sultanahmet, and Beyazıt areas have more modest hotels, as well as family-run *pansiyons* (guest houses) and the popular government-run pansiyons. The trade-off for the simpler quarters is convenience: Staying here makes it easy to return to your hotel at midday or to change before dinner. No matter where you stay, plan ahead: Istanbul has a chronic shortage of beds.

CATEGORY	ISTANBUL*	OTHER AREAS*
$$$$	over $200	over $150
$$$	$100–$200	$100–$150
$$	$60–$100	$50–$100
$	under $60	under $50

* *for two people in a double room, including VAT and service charge*

SOUTH OF THE GOLDEN HORN

$$$$ ★ **ARMADA HOTEL.** Only 10 minutes walk from Istanbul's main tourist sites, the Armada offers spacious, comfortable rooms that have either sea or old city views. One of the hotel's best views is from the terrace of its Ahırkapı restaurant at night. *Ahırkapı, 34400, tel. 212/638–1370, fax 212/518–5060. 110 rooms*

istanbul lodging

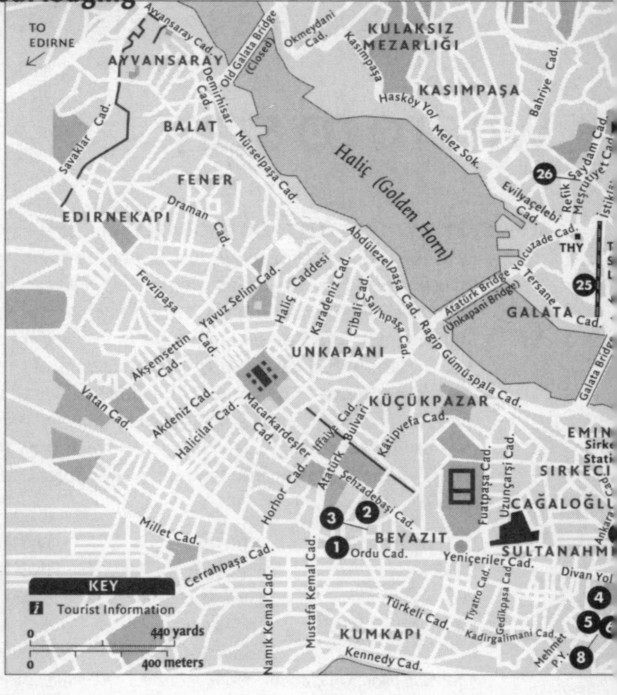

Alp Guest House, 22
Acropol Hotel, 11
Arcadia Hotel, 4
Armada Hotel, 24
Ayasofia Pansiyonları, 15
Berk Guest House, 10
Büyük Londra, 28
Büyük Tarabya, 39
Celal Sultan, 16
Ceylan Inter-Continental, 33
Çırağan Palace, 40
Conrad International İstanbul, 38
Divan Hotel, 34
Fehmi Bey, 6
Four Seasons Hotel, 14
Galata Residence, 25
Hotel Barin, 2
Hotel Empress Zoë, 9
Hotel Nomade, 7
Hotel Residence, 29
Hotel Zürich, 3

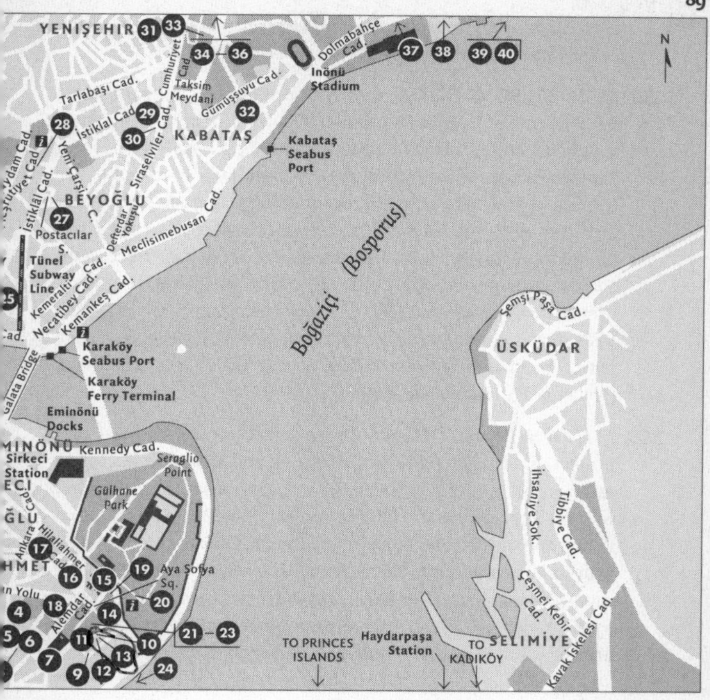

Hyatt Regency, 35
Ibrahim Paşa Oteli, 5
Ishakpasi Konaği, 20
Istanbul Hilton, 36
Konuk Evi, 19
Kybele, 17
Mavi Ev, 23
Merit Antique Hotel, 1
Obelisk Sümengen Hotel, 12
Pera Palace, 26
Richmond Hotel, 27
St. Sophia Hotel, 18
Sari Konak Oteli, 13
Savoy, 30
Sed Hotel, 32
Swissôtel Istanbul, 37
Taksim Plaza Hotel, 31
Turkoman Hotel, 8
Yeşil Ev, 21

with bath. 3 restaurants, bar, room service. AE, MC, V. *www.armadahotel.com.tr*

$$$$ ★ FOUR SEASONS HOTEL. A former prison, this elegant hotel became one of Istanbul's premier accommodations the instant it opened in 1996. This neoclassical building is only steps from Topkapı Palace and the Aya Sofya. Rooms and suites overlook either the Sea of Marmara or an interior courtyard and are luxuriously outfitted with reading chairs, original works of art, and tile bathrooms with deep tubs. The glass-enclosed courtyard restaurant serves both international cuisine and local specialties. Service is exceptional. *Tevkifhane Sok. 1, Sultanahmet, 34490, tel. 212/638–8200, fax 212/638–8530. 65 rooms with bath. Restaurant, bar, room service, health club, business services.* AE, DC, MC, V. *www.fourseasons.com/locations/Istanbul/index.html*

$$$ AYASOFIA PANSIYONLARI. These guest houses are part of a project undertaken by Turkey's Touring and Automobile Club to restore a little street of 19th-century wooden houses along the outer wall of Topkapı Palace. One house has been converted into a library and the rest into pansiyons, furnished in late Ottoman style with Turkish carpets and kilims, brass beds, and big armoires. Front rooms have a view of Aya Sofya, but the rest do not; so if you want a view, specify when you reserve. In summer, tea and refreshments are served in the small courtyard. *Soğukçeşme Sok., Sultanahmet, 34400, tel. 212/513–3660, fax 212/513–3669. 57 rooms with bath. Restaurant, bar, café, Turkish bath.* AE, MC, V. *www.ayasofyapansiyonlari.com.tr*

$$$ MAVI EV (Blue House Hotel). In the heart of the old city, this hotel has an eccentric blue wood façade and clean but slightly dowdily decorated rooms with a 1950s feel. Its rooftop terrace restaurant offers a stunning panorama across the Bosporus and Sea of Marmara and a breathtaking nighttime view of the floodlighted Blue Mosque. *Dalbastı Sok. 14, Sultanahmet, 34490, tel. 212/638–9010, fax 212/638–9017. 27 rooms with bath. 3 restaurants, 2 bars.* AE, MC, V. *www.bluehouse.com.tr*

$$$ MERIT ANTIQUE HOTEL. Four turn-of-the-century apartment buildings were combined to create this hotel. Rooms are generic and unimpressive, but the public spaces couldn't be grander, with arched-glass canopies and reproduction furnishings in turn-of-the-century style. There's even a small stream stocked with goldfish running through the lobby. The only drawback is the neighborhood, on the old-town side, which is mostly full of cheap hotels and restaurants. *Ordu Cad. 226, Laleli, 34470, tel. 212/513–9300, fax 212/512–6390. 247 rooms with bath. 4 restaurants, bar, pool, health club. AE, MC, V. www.meritantiquehotel.com.tr*

$$$ OBELISK SÜMENGEN HOTEL. As its name suggests, this converted Ottoman house with a yellow-and-white-painted wooden facade is just a stone's throw from the obelisks in the Hippodrome. Most rooms are functionally furnished with parquet floors, although some have brass bedsteads and views across the Sea of Marmara. If you fail to locate one of the latter, you can always enjoy the breathtaking panorama from the terrace, where meals are served in warm weather. *Amiral Tafdil Sokak 21, Mimar Mehmet Ağa Cad., Sultanahmet, 34490, tel. 212/517–7173, fax 212/517–6861. 71 rooms with bath. 2 restaurants, bar, Turkish bath. AE, MC, V. www.obelisksumengen.com*

$$$ ★ YEŞIL EV (Green House). Another Touring and Automobile Club project, this lovely old house is on the edge of a small park between the Blue Mosque and Aya Sofya. The hotel is decorated in Ottoman style, with lace curtains and latticed shutters; rooms have brass beds and carved wooden furniture upholstered in velvet or silk (but they're small, with smallish baths and no phones or televisions). The hotel also has a delightful small garden, built around a marble fountain, where you can have breakfast in the warmer weather. *Kabasakal Cad. 5, Sultanahmet, 34400, tel. 212/517–6786, fax 212/517–6780. 19 rooms with bath. Restaurant. AE, MC, V.*

$$ ARCADIA HOTEL. Tucked away in one of the quieter streets in Sultanahmet, this modern hotel's standout feature is its rooftop

terrace with a stunning panoramic view, from the Sea of Marmara to the Blue Mosque and Aya Sofya, which is simply entrancing at night. *Dr. İmran Öktem Cad. 1, Sultanahmet, 34400, tel. 212/516–9696, fax 212/516–6118. 42 rooms with bath, 6 suites. Restaurant. AE, MC, V.*

$$ ACROPOL HOTEL. Another restored Ottoman house, in the quaintly named "White Mustache Street" offers rooms that combine rather cumbersome imitation period furniture with modern conveniences. Few, except for the suites, have much of a view, although the rooftop restaurant more than compensates. *Akbıyık Cad. 25, Sultanahmet, 34400, tel. 212/638–9021, fax 212/518–3031. 24 rooms with bath, 2 suites. Restaurant. AE, MC, V. www.acropolhotel.com*

$$ CELAL SULTAN. A restored town house, which opened as a hotel in 1996, the Celal Sultan has hardwood floors and kilims that give rooms a sense of warmth and quiet sophistication. From the rooftop terrace you can enjoy a fine view of the Blue Mosque and the Sea of Marmara. Unusual for Istanbul, the water in the hotel is filtered. The proprietor, Mr. Selami, and his wife are full of good sightseeing and shopping tips. *Salkımsöğüt Sok. 16, Yerebatan Cad., Sultanahmet, 34410, tel. 212/520–9323, fax 212/522–9724. 30 rooms with bath, 2 suites. Restaurant. AE, MC, V. www.istanbulhotels.com/celalsultan.htm*

$$ FEHMI BEY. In a beautifully restored and refurbished old town house just off the Hippodrome, this hotel is adorned with owner Fehmi Bey's antiques and kilims. After a long day of sightseeing, the sauna and rooftop terrace bar with views of the old city relax and restore both body and soul. *Üçler Sok. 15, Sultanahmet, 34440, tel. 212/638–9083, fax 212/518–1264. 34 rooms with bath. Sauna. AE, MC, V.*

$$ HOTEL BARIN. Modern, clean, and comfortable, this hotel makes up for in convenience, functionality, and a friendly staff what it lacks in atmosphere. It attracts a large number of business travelers as well as tourists. *Fevziye Cad. 7, Şehzadebaşı, 34470, tel. 212/513–9100, fax 212/526–4440. 65 rooms with bath. Restaurant. AE, MC, V. www.barinhotel.com*

$$ HOTEL ZÜRICH. This 10-story hotel is efficient, well run, and one of the best options in the Laleli neighborhood (most other choices are rather shabby). The lobby is highly polished, and rooms are bright and carpeted and have little balconies. Ask for one of the higher floors; they're quieter. *Harikzadeler Sok. 37, Laleli, 34470, tel. 212/512–2350, fax 212/526–9731. 132 rooms with bath. Restaurant, 2 bars, nightclub, pool. MC, V. www.akturkhotels.com/hotelzurich*

$$ IBRAHIM PAŞA OTELI. This French-owned hotel in an exquisitely renovated Ottoman house in the historic Sultanahmet neighborhood has a rooftop terrace with glorious views of the Blue Mosque. Though rooms are small and simple, the lobby and bar downstairs, where you can have a wonderful breakfast, are warmly decorated and comfortable. The personable staff ensures a relaxing atmosphere. *Terzihane Sok. 5, Sultanahmet, 34400, tel. 212/518–0394 or 212/518–0395, fax 212/518–4457. 19 rooms with bath. Bar. AE, MC, V. www.all-hotels.com/a/tkpasha/tkpasha.htm*

$$ KONUK EVI. Under the same management as its larger neighbor Ayasofia Pansiyonları, with which it shares contact details, this former Ottoman mansion has been restored with period furnishings, from the large brass mirrors and crystal chandeliers in the lobby to brass bedsteads and velvet curtains in the high-ceilinged rooms. In the summer meals are served in a delightful little garden. *Soğukçeşme Sok., Sultanahmet, 34400, tel. 212/513–3660, fax 212/513–3669. 10 rooms with bath, 2 suites. Restaurant, bar. AE, MC, V. www.ayasofyapansiyonlari.com.tr*

$$ KYBELE. Named after an ancient Anatolian fertility goddess, the Kybele has numerous fascinating features, including a lobby lighted by 1,002 lamps, antique furniture, kilims, and calligraphic plates. Rooms have dark-wood furniture and bare walls, and

some have kilims. *Yerebatan Cad. 35, Sultanahmet, 34410, tel. 212/511–7766, fax 212/513–4393. 16 rooms with bath. Bar. AE, MC, V. www.kybelehotel.com*

$$ ST. SOPHIA HOTEL. This member of the Best Western International chain combines comfortable, tastefully decorated rooms with a full range of modern facilities and a very helpful staff. *Alemdar Caddesi 2, Sultanahmet, 34400, tel. 212/528–0974, fax 212/511–5491. 25 rooms with bath, 2 suites. Restaurant, bar. AE, MC, V. www.istanbulhotels.com/stsophia*

$$ SARI KONAK OTELI. This small, family-run hotel in an Ottoman-style building provides a very comfortable stay. The decor throughout is modern, but with Turkish tilework accents and an old, intricately paneled door at the front desk. From your room's tiny balcony with lattice shutters, lean out to hear the call to prayer echoing in Sultanahmet. If you don't want twin beds, and prefer a bathtub to a shower, say so when making reservations. On the rooftop terrace, you can sip a glass of rakı and contemplate either the Marmara Sea or the nearby Blue Mosque's spires. A treat in the morning is the delicious mix of yogurt, cereal, and dried fruits that's part of the Continental buffet. *Mimar Mehmet Aga Cad. 42–46, Sultanahmet, 34400, tel. 212/638–6258, fax 212/517–8635. 17 rooms. Breakfast room, air-conditioning (some), fans, in-room safes, minibars, non-smoking rooms, room service, laundry services, travel services. AE, MC, V. CP. www.sarikonak.com*

$$ TURKOMAN HOTEL. This restored Ottoman house has a spacious lobby and simple, clean rooms with brass beds, old carpets and attractive wooden furniture. Ask for a room looking out over Aya Sofya. The terrace, where breakfast is served in summer, has a fine view over the Sea of Marmara. *Asmalı Çeşme Sok. 2, Sultanahmet, 34400, tel. 212/516–2956, fax 212/516–2957. 20 rooms with bath. Bar AE, MC, V. www.turkomanhotel.com*

$ ALP GUEST HOUSE. This small, clean hotel is in the heart of the old city and has comfortable, simply furnished rooms. The terrace offers fine views of the Blue Mosque and the Sea of Marmara. Airport pickup service is available on request. *Adliye Sok. 4, Akbıyık Cad., Sultanahmet, 34490, tel. 212/517–9570, fax 212/638–3922. 12 rooms with bath. MC, V. www.alpguesthouse.com*

$ **BERK GUEST HOUSE.** Cheerful Güngör and Nevin Evrensel run this clean, comfortable pansiyon in a converted private home. There are a small lounge inside and a terrace with beautiful views across the Sea of Marmara. Two of the rooms also have balconies overlooking a garden. *Kutluğün Sok. 27, Sultanahmet, 34400, tel. 212/516–9671, fax 212/517–7715. 9 rooms with bath. AE, V. www.berkguesthouse.com*

$ ★ **HOTEL EMPRESS ZOË.** This small, unusual hotel with a friendly staff is near the sights in Sultanahmet. Named for the 11th-century empress who was one of the few women to rule Byzantium, it is decorated in the style of that period. The terrace bar offers fine panoramic views of the old city, and breakfast is served in the garden or indoors. Rooms are accented with colorful textiles; a couple have terraces, and some are very small. Note that to get up to rooms you must climb a spiral staircase. The American owner, Ann Nevans, can help you with your itinerary. *Akbıyık Cad., Adliye Sok. 10, Sultanahmet, 34400, tel. 212/518–4360, fax 212/518–5699. 14 rooms with bath, 2 suites, 1 penthouse. MC, V. www.emzoe.com*

$ ★ **HOTEL NOMADE.** The service is personal, the beds comfortable, and the prices low at this Sultanahmet pansiyon. The building is a restored five-story Ottoman house decorated with kilims and folk crafts. Rooms are small but the roof-garden bar and terrace have views of Sultanahmet. *Ticarethane Sok. 15, Sultanahmet, 34400, tel. 212/511–1296 or 212/513–8172, fax 212/513–2404. 15 rooms with bath. AE, MC, V. www.book-hotel.com/nomade*

$ ★ **İSHAKPAŞI KONAĞI.** This little timber-face pansiyon has small, clean, simply furnished rooms and looks out toward the walls of Topkapı Palace. In warm weather, breakfast is served in a pleasant

garden. *İakpaşı 15, Sultanahmet, 34400, tel. 212/638–6267 or 212/638–6027, fax 212/638–1870. 19 rooms with bath. AE, MC, V.*

BEYOĞLU AREA

$$$ GALATA RESIDENCE. This hotel is in the oldest apartment building in Istanbul, built in 1881 for the Camondos, one of the leading banking families of the late Ottoman Empire. Rooms have been carefully furnished with period furniture, supplemented discretely with modern conveniences such as bathtubs and air-conditioning. Prices of the one- and two-bedroom apartments, which come with kitchenettes, compare very favorably with rooms at Istanbul's upscale hotels, many of which have only a fraction of the Galata's character. Apartments on the upper floors and the top-floor restaurant have excellent views across the Golden Horn to the old city. *Felek Sok. 2, Bankalar Cad., Galata, 80020, tel. 212/292–4841, fax 212/244–2323. 15 apartments. Restaurant, café, air-conditioning, kitchenettes. AE, DC, MC, V. www.galataresidence.com*

$$$ PERA PALACE. Built in 1892 to accommodate guests arriving on the *Orient Express*, this hotel is full of atmosphere. Everyone who was anyone in the late 19th and early 20th centuries stayed here, from Mata Hari to numerous heads of state. The rooms once occupied by Kemal Atatürk and Agatha Christie have been turned into museums. The elevator looks like a gilded bird cage, the main stairway is white marble, and the lobby surrounding it has 20-ft-high coral-marble walls. Unfortunately, though the hotel has been modernized, its facilities and rooms are not in the greatest shape, making it a favorite of romantics rather than those who need a full range of modern amenities. *Meşrutiyet Cad. 98, Tepebaşı, 80050, tel. 212/251–4560, fax 212/251–4089. 145 rooms with bath. Restaurant, bar, café. AE, DC, MC, V. www.perapalas.com*

$$ BÜYÜK LONDRA. This six-story structure, built in the 1850s as the home of a wealthy Italian family, has grown old gracefully. Rooms are small and comfortably worn, and the current layout has the feel of an old apartment building. The dark woods and velvet drapes used in the high-ceiling lobby and dining room exude an aura of the Ottoman Victorian era. *Meşrutiyet Cad. 117, Tepebaşı, 80050, tel. 212/293–1619, fax 212/245–0671. 54 rooms with bath. Restaurant. AE, MC, V.*

$$ RICHMOND HOTEL. On pedestrian İstiklal Caddesi, very close to the consulates, this hotel occupies a turn-of-the-century building. Rooms are plush and clean; some have views of the Bosporus. The sidewalk patisserie Lebon at the entrance is a remake of the original. *İstiklal Cad. 445, 80070, tel. 212/252–5460 or 212/252–9852, fax 212/252–9707. 109 rooms with bath. Restaurant, bar, café, meeting room. AE, V. www.richmondhotels.com*

$ HOTEL RESIDENCE. On bustling İstiklal Caddesi, the rooms here are simple, comfortable, and clean, if a little lacking in character. Ask for room at the back, as those overlooking the street tend to be noisy very late into the night. *Alışık Sok. 19, İstiklal Caddesi, 80070, tel. 212/252–7685, fax 212/243–0084. 52 rooms with bath. Bar. MC, V.*

TAKSIM SQUARE

$$$$ CEYLAN INTER-CONTINENTAL. Until the mid-1990s, when its lease ran out, this hotel was the Istanbul Sheraton. Extensively refurbished into a plush luxury hotel under its new owners, the Inter-Continental has rapidly become one of Turkey's premier accommodations, with a broad range of top-class facilities. Rooms on the Bosporus side have excellent views. *Askerocağı Cad. 1, Taksim, 80200, tel. 212/231–2121, 800/327–0200 in the U.S., 0345/581–444 in the U.K.; fax 212/231–2180. 390 rooms, 55 suites with bath. 3 restaurants, 3 bars, pool, health club. AE, DC, MC, V. www.interconti.com*

$$$$ HYATT REGENCY. This massive but tastefully designed pink building recalls Ottoman splendor. So does the interior, with its plush carpeting and earthy tones. Rooms have views of the Bosporus and the Taksim district. *Taşkıla Cad., Taksim, 80900, tel. 212/225–7000; 800/228–9000 in the U.S.; fax 212/225–7007. 360 rooms* *with bath. 3 restaurants, 3 bars, café, pool, beauty salon, Turkish bath, health club, business services, baby-sitting. AE, DC, MC, V. www.istanbul.hyatt.com*

$$$$ ISTANBUL HILTON. Lavishly decorated with white marble, Turkish rugs, and large brass urns, this is one of the best Hiltons in the chain. The extensive grounds, filled with rosebushes, make the hotel a restful haven in a bustling city. Rooms are Hilton standard, with plush carpeting and pastel decor; ask for one with a view of the Bosporus. *Cumhuriyet Cad., Harbiye, 80200, tel. 212/231–4650; 800/445–8667 in the U.S.; fax 212/240–4165. 501 rooms with bath. 4 restaurants, 2 bars, indoor pool, pool, spa, Turkish bath, 3 tennis courts, health club, squash, shops. AE, DC, MC, V. www.hilton.com*

$$$ DIVAN HOTEL. The staff at this quiet, modern hotel is thoroughly professional. The restaurant is excellent, and the public spaces and good-size rooms are comfortable if a little dowdy. *Cumhuriyet Cad. 2, Taksim, 80200, tel. 212/231–4100, fax 212/248–8527. 180 rooms with bath. 2 restaurants, bar, tea shop, pool. AE, DC, MC. www.divanoteli.com.tr*

$$$ TAKSIM PLAZA HOTEL. This upmarket hotel in the center of Taksim is a favorite with visiting executives. Its rooms are modern and well-appointed, and it has an elegant lobby and restaurant. *Topçu Cad. 8, Taksim, 80090, tel. 212/238–9220, fax 212/238–9238. 142 rooms with bath. Restaurant, bar, sauna. AE, MC, V.*

$$ SAVOY. This modern 10-story hotel is centrally located in the heart of the new town, with comfortably furnished rooms and marble-lined bathrooms. Rooms at the front look out over Taksim Square, which can be lively into the early hours, while those on upper floors at the back have views across the Bosporus. *Sıraselviler Cad. 29, Taksim, 80060, tel. 212/252–9326, fax 212/243–2010. 80 rooms with bath, 10 suites. Restaurant, bar. AE, MC, V. www.savoy.com.tr*

BOSPORUS

$$$$ **ÇIRAĞAN PALACE.** This 19th-century Ottoman palace (pronounced
★ Shi-rahn) is the city's most luxurious hotel. The setting is exceptional—right on the Bosporus, the outdoor pool is on the water's edge. The public spaces are all done up in cool marble and rich tones. Rooms have Ottoman-inspired wood furnishings and textiles in warm colors (ask for a renovated one); views are exceptional. Most rooms are in the new wing, though there are 12 suites in the palace. *Çırağan Cad. 84, Beşiktaş, 80700, tel. 212/258–3377, fax 212/259–6686. 287 rooms, 28 suites with bath. 4 restaurants, bar, indoor pool, pool, Turkish bath, health club. AE, DC, MC, V. www.ciragan.com*

$$$$ **CONRAD INTERNATIONAL ISTANBUL.** This modern 14-story tower, catering primarily to business travelers, has spectacular views of the Bosporus and terraced gardens. Rooms are tastefully furnished with all the amenities expected of an international hotel. The staff is congenial and efficient. *Barbaros Bul. 46, Beşiktaş, 80700, tel. 212/227–3000, fax 212/259–6667. 620 rooms with bath. 3 restaurants, 2 bars, indoor pool, pool, 2 tennis courts, health club, shops, business services. AE, DC, MC, V. www.hilton.com/conradinternational/hotels/ISTHCCI/index.html*

$$$$ **SWISSÔTEL ISTANBUL.** In a superb spot just above Dolmabahçe
★ Palace, this hotel was controversial—nobody liked the idea of such a big, modern structure towering over the palace. But you'll appreciate its views—all the way to Topkapı Palace across the Golden Horn. The vast, high-ceiling lobby is usually filled with the sound of a tinkling piano. The occasional Swiss-village mural strikes a jarring note in Istanbul, but service is crisp and efficient. Rooms, done in muted greens, have contemporary if undistinguished furnishings. *Bayıldım Cad. 2, Maçka, 80680, tel. 212/326–1100, fax 212/326–1122. 600 rooms with bath. 7 restaurants, 3*

Hotel How-Tos

Where you stay does make a difference. Do you prefer a modern high-rise or an intimate B&B? A center-city location or the quiet suburbs? What facilities do you want? Sort through your priorities, then price it all out.

HOW TO GET A DEAL After you've chosen a likely candidate or two, phone them directly and price a room for your travel dates. Then call the hotel's toll-free number and ask the same questions. Also try consolidators and hotel-room discounters. You won't hear the same rates twice. On the spot, make a reservation as soon as you are quoted a price you want to pay.

PROMISES, PROMISES If you have special requests, make them when you reserve. Get written confirmation of any promises.

SETTLE IN Upon arriving, make sure everything works—lights and lamps, TV and radio, sink, tub, shower, and anything else that matters. Report any problems immediately. And don't wait until you need extra pillows or blankets or an ironing board to call housekeeping. Also check out the fire emergency instructions. Know where to find the fire exits, and make sure your companions do, too.

IF YOU NEED TO COMPLAIN Be polite but firm. Explain the problem to the person in charge. Suggest a course of action. If you aren't satisfied, repeat your requests to the manager. Document everything: Take pictures and keep a written record of who you've spoken with, when, and what was said. Contact your travel agent, if he made the reservations.

KNOW THE SCORE When you go out, take your hotel's business cards (one for everyone in your party). If you have extras, you can give them out to new acquaintances who want to call you.

TIP UP FRONT For special services, a tip or partial tip in advance can work wonders.

USE ALL THE HOTEL RESOURCES A concierge can make difficult things easy. But a desk clerk, bellhop, or other hotel employee who's friendly, smart, and ambitious can often steer you straight as well. A gratuity is in order if the advice is helpful.

bars, indoor pool, pool, health club, business services. AE, DC, MC, V. www.swissotel.com

$$$ BÜYÜK TARABYA. This summer resort, less than an hour's drive up the Bosporus from the center of Istanbul, is popular with more affluent locals. Though it has been around for years, it is well maintained and perfectly modern, with bright white walls and plenty of cool marble. It has a private beach. *Kefeliköy Cad., Tarabya, tel. 212/262–1000, fax 212/262–2260. 267 rooms with bath. Restaurant, bar, indoor pool, pool, health club, beach. AE, MC, V.*

$$ SED HOTEL. Tucked away on a side street, halfway down the hill from Taksim Square to Kabataş, the Sed makes up for being slightly off the tourist track by providing superb Bosporus views from many of its rooms at half the price of a five-star hotel. It also has a good restaurant. Insist on a room with a view. *Beşaret Sok. 14, Ayapaşa, 80040, tel. 212/252–2710, fax 212/252–4274. 50 rooms with bath. Restaurant, bar. MC, V.*

PRACTICAL INFORMATION

Air Travel

BOOKING

When you book, **look for nonstop flights** and **remember that "direct" flights stop at least once.** Try to avoid connecting flights, which require a change of plane.

CARRIERS

Although THY/Turkish Airlines, the national flag carrier of Turkey, may offer the most nonstops, an international carrier based in your home country is more likely to have better connections to your hometown and serve a greater number of gateway cities. Third-country carriers (a foreign carrier based in a country other than your own or Turkey) sometimes offer the lowest fares.

Try to **arrive at the airport at least an hour and a half before takeoff** because security checks at the entrance to the terminal can be time consuming; checked luggage must be identified by boarding passengers before it is put on the plane, and all unidentified luggage is left behind and checked for bombs or firearms. At most airports you will be asked to **show your passport** before you are allowed to check in.

➤ **MAJOR AIRLINES:** From the U.S.: **Air Canada** (tel. 800/776–3000). **Air France** (tel. 800/237–2747). **British Airways** (tel. 800/247–9297). **Delta** (tel. 800/241–4141). **Lufthansa** (tel. 800/645–3880). **Northwest/KLM** (tel. 800/447–4747). **Olympic Airlines** (tel. 800/223–1226). **Swissair** (tel. 800/221–4750). **THY/Turkish Airlines** (tel. 212/339–9650; 800/874–8875; 212/252–1106 in Istanbul; 212/663–6363 for reservations). **TWA** (tel. 800/221–2000 in the U.S.; 800/892–4141).

➤ **FROM CANADA:** **Air Canada** (tel. 800/776–3000). **British Airways** (tel. 800/247–9297). **Air France** (tel. 800/237–2747). **Alitalia** (tel. 800/223–5730). **Finnair** (tel. 800/950–5000). **KLM** (tel. 800/374–

7747). **Lufthansa** (tel. 800/645–3880). **Olympic Air** (tel. 800/223–1226). **SAS** (tel. 800/221–2350). **Swissair** (tel. 800/221–4750). **TWA** (tel. 800/221–2000 or 800/892–4141).

➤ FROM THE U.K.: **British Airways** (tel. 020/8897–4000; 0345/222–111 outside London). **Lufthansa** (tel. 0345/737–747). **Turkish Airlines** (11–12 Hanover St., London W1R 9HF, tel. 020/7499–9249 or 020/7499–4499).

FLYING TIMES

The flying time to Istanbul is 10 hours from New York, 13 hours from Chicago, and 15 hours from Los Angeles. The flight from Toronto to Istanbul takes 11½ hours. Flying time from London is 4 hours.

Airport & Transfers

AIRPORT

Turkey's major airport is Atatürk Airport, about 18 km (12 mi) from Istanbul.

➤ AIRPORT INFORMATION: **Atatürk Airport** (tel. 212/663–6400).

TRANSFERS

Shuttle buses make the 30- to 40-minute trip from the airport's international and domestic terminals—which are some distance apart—to the Turkish Airlines office in Taksim Square; buses to the airport depart from Taksim Square every hour from 6 AM until 11 PM and as demand warrants after that. Allow at least 45 minutes for the bus ride in this direction. Taxis, which are metered, charge about $15 to Taksim Square and $11 to Sultanahmet Square.

➤ INFORMATION: **Shuttle bus** (tel. 212/252–1106).

Boat & Ferry Travel

Istanbul is well served by ferries; the main docks are at Eminönü, on the Old Stamboul side of the Galata Bridge;

Karaköy, on the other side of the bridge; Kabataş, near Dolmabahçe Palace; and across the Bosporus on the Asian shore, at Üsküdar and Kadiköy.

Commuter ferries crisscross between these points day and night and provide great views at a most reasonable price (usually $3 or less round-trip). Information on all city ferries is available between 9 and 5 from the Istanbul Ferry Lines office. The *deniz otobüsü* (sea buses), which are large, powerful catamarans painted blue, red, and white, are practical and speedy and operate to and from Karaköy, Kadıköy, Kabataş, Bostancı, the Princes Islands, Yalova, and Bakırköy. Schedules are available at docks marked DENIZ OTOBÜSÜ TERMINALI and are also available on a 24-hour Turkish-language telephone service.

Best for sightseeing is the Anadolu Kavağı boat, which makes all the stops on the European and Asian sides of the Bosporus. It leaves year-round from the Eminönü Docks, Pier 5, next to the Galata Bridge on the Old Stamboul side, at 10:35 and 1:35, with two extra trips on weekdays and four extra trips on Sunday from April through August. Unless you speak Turkish, have your hotel call for boat schedules, as English is rarely spoken at the docks. The round-trip fare is $6; the ride each way lasts one hour and 45 minutes. You can disembark at any of the stops and pick up a later boat, or return by taxi, dolmuş, or bus.

➤ **BOAT & FERRY INFORMATION: Anadolu Kavağı** (tel. 212/522–0045). **Deniz Otobüsü Terminalı** (tel. 216/362–0444). **Istanbul Ferry Lines** (tel. 212/244–4233).

Bus Travel Around Istanbul

The city's buses (mostly vermilion and blue) and trams are crowded and slow, but they are useful for getting around and—at about 50¢ per ride—inexpensive. The route name and number are posted on the front of each vehicle; curbside signboards list routes and itineraries. Buy tickets before boarding; they're available individually and in books of 10 from ticket stands near each stop or from newsstands around the city, and for a few cents above face value, they can also be purchased from shoeshine boys and men sitting on wooden crates at most bus stops. London-style double-deckers operate between Sultanahmet and Emirgan on the Bosporus and between Taksim and Bostancı on the Asian side. Unlike the older city buses, these are clean and offer a panoramic ride. A bus attendant collects fares of three individual tickets (totaling $1.50).

Bus Travel to and from Istanbul

Buses arrive at the Esenler Otogar (Esenler Station), outside the city near Bayrampaşa. This terminal is accessible by the Hızlı Tren (rapid train) system, which leaves from Aksaray. However, the train is often very crowded, particularly at rush hour, and you might be better off taking a taxi. A few buses from Anatolia arrive at the Harem Terminal, on the Asian side of the Bosporus. Most bus companies have minibus services from the bus terminals to the area around Taksim Square and Aksaray, which is close to many hotels. Private taxis cost about $12 from Esenler Terminal to Taksim or Sultanahmet and about $10 from the Harem Terminal. Note that you'll have to pay the Bosporus Bridge toll when crossing from Asia to Europe, or vice versa.

➤ INFORMATION: **Esenler Otogar** (tel. 212/658–0036). **Harem Terminal** (tel. 216/333–3763).

Business Hours

BANKS & OFFICES

Banks are normally open weekdays from 8:30 until noon or 12:30, depending on the bank, and from 1:30 until 5.

GAS STATIONS

Most gas stations are open from 6 AM to 10 PM, although there can be considerable variation. There are 24-hour gas stations in the city; look for the sign 24 SAAT AÇIK.

MUSEUMS & SIGHTS

Museums are generally open Tuesday through Sunday from 9:30 AM until 5 or 5:30 PM and closed on Monday. Palaces are open the same hours but are generally closed Thursday. Many museums stop selling tickets 30 minutes before the actual closing time. Sometimes this is explicitly stated in the official times, but very often, particularly away from the major sites, it is unofficial and just a way for museum staffers to make sure they get away on time. To be on the safe side, try to ensure that you arrive at least 45 minutes before closing time.

SHOPS

Shops and bazaars are usually open Monday through Saturday from 9:30 to 7 and closed on Sunday. However, in tourist areas, shops may stay open until 9 PM and all day Sunday. All large stores remain open throughout the day, though some small shops close for lunch between 1 and 2.

Cameras & Photography

➤ **PHOTO HELP: Kodak Information Center** (tel. 800/242–2424). ***Kodak Guide to Shooting Great Travel Pictures*,** available in bookstores or from Fodor's Travel Publications (tel. 800/533–6478; $18.00 plus $5.50 shipping).

Car Rental

Rates begin at $35 a day and $250 a week for an economy car with unlimited mileage. Gas costs about 75¢ per liter. The majority of rental cars are stick shift, though it is possible to get an automatic with advance arrangements. A wide variety of mostly European car makes are available, ranging from the locally manufactured Tofaş (a subsidiary of Fiat) to Renault and Mercedes.

➤ **MAJOR AGENCIES: Alamo** (tel. 800/522–9696; 020/8759–6200 in the U.K.). **Avis** (tel. 800/331–1084; 800/331–1084 in Canada; 02/9353–9000 in Australia; 09/525–1982 in New Zealand). **Budget** (tel. 800/527–0700;0870/607–5000 in the U.K., through affiliate Europcar). **Dollar** (tel. 800/800–6000; 0124/622–0111 in the U.K., through affiliate Sixt Kenning; 02/9223–1444 in Australia). **Hertz** (tel. 800/654–3001; 800/263–0600 in Canada; 020/8897–2072 in the U.K.; 02/9669–2444 in Australia; 09/256–8690 in New Zealand). **National Car Rental** (tel. 800/227–7368; 020/8680–4800 in the U.K., where it is known as National Europe).

INSURANCE

When driving a rented car, you are generally responsible for any damage to or loss of the vehicle as well as for any property damage or personal injury that you may cause. Many agencies provide optional insurance for an extra charge; before you opt for such extra insurance, see what coverage your personal auto-insurance policy and credit cards already provide.

REQUIREMENTS & RESTRICTIONS

In Turkey, a driver's license issued in most foreign countries is acceptable.

SURCHARGES

Before arranging to pick up a car in one city and leave it in another, **ask about drop-off charges or one-way service fees,** which can be substantial. Note, too, that some rental agencies charge extra if you return the car before the time specified in your contract. To avoid a hefty refueling fee, **fill the tank just before you turn in the car,** but be aware that gas stations near the rental outlet may overcharge.

Car Travel

Turkey has one of the world's highest auto accident rates and driving in Istanbul is best avoided. **Be extremely careful when passing,** even on roads that have a designated third lane for doing so. You should also **avoid driving on highways after dusk** because drivers often don't turn their lights on. Vehicles may be stopped on the roads in complete darkness.

E80 runs between Istanbul and central Anatolia to the east; this toll road is the best of several alternatives. You can also enter or leave the city on one of the numerous car ferries that ply the Sea of Marmara from the Kabataş docks. There's an overnight ferry to İzmir from the Eminönü docks. To get out of the city by car, your best bet is to buy a map, as the signs aren't always so clear.

AUTO CLUBS

➤ **In Australia: Australian Automobile Association** (tel. 02/6247–7311).

➤ **In Canada: Canadian Automobile Association** (CAA; tel. 613/247–0117).

➤ **In New Zealand: New Zealand Automobile Association** (tel. 09/377–4660).

➤ **In the U.K.: Automobile Association** (AA; tel. 0990/500–600). **Royal Automobile Club** (RAC; tel. 0990/722–722 for membership; 0345/121–345 for insurance).

➤ **In the U.S.: American Automobile Association** (tel. 800/564–6222).

EMERGENCY SERVICES

A road rescue service is available on some highways; **before you embark on a journey, ask your car rental agency or hotel how to contact it in case of an emergency.** Most major car manufacturers in Turkey (for example, Renault, Fiat, and Opel/General Motors) also have roaming 24-hour services.

Most Turkish gas stations have at least one staff member with some knowledge of car mechanics who can diagnose problems and provide "first aid" or advice, such as directions to the nearest mechanic. If a gas station attendant fixes a minor problem, it is customary to give him a small tip of about $5–$10 depending on the time and effort expended.

In Istanbul, entire streets are given over to car-repair shops run by teams of experts—one specializes in radiators, another in electrical fittings, and another in steering columns. It's not expensive to have repairs done, but it's customary to give a small tip to the person who does the repairs. If you don't want to wait for the work to be done, **take all car documents with you when you leave the shop.**

GASOLINE

Shell, British Petroleum, Total, Elf, and two Turkish oil companies, Petrol Ofisi and Türkpetrol, operate stations in Turkey. Many of those on the main highways stay open around the clock, others from 6 AM to 10 PM.

ROAD CONDITIONS

Signposts are few, lighting scarce, and city traffic chaotic. Urban streets and highways are jammed with vehicles operated by high-speed lunatics and drivers who constantly honk their horns. **Avoid the many small one-way streets**—you never know when someone is going to barrel down one of them in the wrong direction.

RULES OF THE ROAD

In general, Turkish driving conforms to Mediterranean customs, with driving on the right and passing on the left. **Be prepared for drivers to do anything.** Seatbelts are required for front-seat passengers and a good idea for those in back seats. Using a cellular phone while driving is prohibited—but this law is seldom obeyed.

Children in Istanbul

Turkey is not the easiest place to travel with young children, as there are few child-oriented facilities. However, Turks are traditionally very fond of children, and are eager to be of assistance. Restaurants are generally casual and accommodating to families, and diapers and baby food are easy to find.

LODGING

Most hotels in Istanbul allow children under a certain age to stay in their parents' room at no extra charge, but others charge for them as extra adults. In general, you can't count on Turkish hotels to have cribs or cots, so be sure to request them in advance.

SIGHTS & ATTRACTIONS

Places that are especially appealing to children are indicated by a rubber duckie icon in the margin.

Customs & Duties

When shopping, **keep receipts** for all purchases. Upon reentering the country, **be ready to show customs officials what you've bought.** If you feel a duty is incorrect or object to the way your clearance was handled, note the inspector's badge number and ask to see a supervisor. If the problem isn't resolved, write to the appropriate authorities, beginning with the port director at your point of entry.

IN TURKEY

Turkish customs officials rarely look through tourists' luggage on arrival. You are allowed to bring in 400 cigarettes, 50 cigars, 200 grams of tobacco, 1½ kilograms of instant coffee, 500 grams of tea, and 2½ liters of alcohol. Items in the duty-free shops in Turkish airports, for international arrivals, are usually less expensive than they are in European airports or in flight.

IN AUSTRALIA

Australian residents who are 18 or older may bring home $A400 worth of souvenirs and gifts (including jewelry), 250 cigarettes or 250 grams of tobacco, and 1,125 milliliters of alcohol (including wine, beer, and spirits). Residents under 18 may bring back $A200 worth of goods. Prohibited items include meat products. Seeds, plants, and fruits need to be declared upon arrival.

➤ INFORMATION: **Australian Customs Service** (Regional Director, Box 8, Sydney, NSW 2001, tel. 02/9213–2000, fax 02/9213–4000, www.customs.gov.au).

IN CANADA

Canadian residents who have been out of Canada for at least 7 days may bring home C$500 worth of goods duty-free. If you've been away less than 7 days but more than 48 hours, the duty-free allowance drops to C$200; if your trip lasts 24–48 hours, the allowance is C$50. You may not pool allowances with family members. Goods claimed under the C$500 exemption may follow you by mail; those claimed under the lesser exemptions must accompany you. Alcohol and tobacco products may be included in the 7-day and 48-hour exemptions but not in the 24-hour exemption. If you meet the age requirements of the province or territory through which you reenter Canada, you may bring in, duty-free, 1.14 liters (40 imperial ounces) of wine or liquor *or* 24 12-ounce cans or bottles of beer or ale. If you are 16 or older, you may bring in, duty-free, 200 cigarettes and 50 cigars. Check ahead of time with Revenue Canada or the Department of Agriculture for policies regarding meat products, seeds, plants, and fruits.

You may send an unlimited number of gifts worth up to C$60 each duty-free to Canada. Label the package UNSOLICITED GIFT—VALUE UNDER $60. Alcohol and tobacco are excluded.

➤ INFORMATION: **Revenue Canada** (2265 St. Laurent Blvd. S, Ottawa, Ontario K1G 4K3, tel. 613/993–0534; 800/461–9999 in Canada, fax 613/991–4126, www.ccra-adrc.gc.ca).

IN NEW ZEALAND

Homeward-bound residents 17 or older may bring back $700 worth of souvenirs and gifts. Your duty-free allowance also includes 4.5 liters of wine or beer; one 1,125-milliliter bottle of spirits; and either 200 cigarettes, 250 grams of tobacco, 50 cigars, or a combination of the three up to 250 grams.

Prohibited items include meat products, seeds, plants, and fruits.

➤ INFORMATION: **New Zealand Customs** (Custom House, 50 Anzac Ave., Box 29, Auckland,, tel. 09/359–6655, fax 09/359–6732).

IN THE U.K.

From countries outside the EU, including Turkey, you may bring home, duty-free, 200 cigarettes or 50 cigars; 1 liter of spirits or 2 liters of fortified or sparkling wine or liqueurs; 2 liters of still table wine; 60 ml of perfume; 250 ml of toilet water; plus £136 worth of other goods, including gifts and souvenirs. If returning from outside the EU, prohibited items include meat products, seeds, plants, and fruits.

➤ INFORMATION: **HM Customs and Excise** (Dorset House, Stamford St., Bromley, Kent BR1 1XX, tel. 020/7202–4227, www.hmce.gov.uk).

IN THE U.S.

U.S. residents who have been out of the country for at least 48 hours (and who have not used the $400 allowance or any part of it in the past 30 days) may bring home $400 worth of foreign goods duty-free.

U.S. residents 21 and older may bring back 1 liter of alcohol duty-free. In addition, regardless of your age, you are allowed 200 cigarettes and 100 non-Cuban cigars. Antiques, which the U.S. Customs Service defines as objects more than 100 years old, enter duty-free, as do original works of art done entirely by hand, including paintings, drawings, and sculptures.

You may also send packages home duty-free: up to $200 worth of goods for personal use, with a limit of one parcel per addressee per day (except alcohol or tobacco products or perfume worth more than $5); label the package PERSONAL USE and attach a list of its contents and their retail value. Do not label the package UNSOLICITED GIFT, or your duty-free exemption will drop to $100. Mailed items do not affect your duty-free allowance on your return.

➤ INFORMATION: **U.S. Customs Service** (1300 Pennsylvania Ave. NW, Washington, DC 20229, www.customs.gov; inquiries tel. 202/354–1000; complaints c/o 1300 Pennsylvania Ave. NW, Room 5.4D, Washington, DC 20229; registration of equipment c/o Resource Management, tel. 202/354–1000).

Dining

You can find restaurants or cafés open almost any time of the day or night. However, lunch is generally served from noon to 3, dinner from 7 to 10. Breakfast starts early, typically by 7. Most Turks fast during daylight hours during the Islamic holy month of Ramadan. During that time many restaurants close during the day and open at dusk.

Disabilities & Accessibility

Unfortunately, Turkey isn't on par with other parts of the world in terms of accessibility. However, many buses have special seats designated for passengers with disabilities, and some "kneel" to make it easier for less-mobile travelers to board. Some museums and upscale hotels have ramps and elevators, but you are less likely to find these in older museums and small pensions. But locals are likely to be very helpful.

Discounts & Deals

DISCOUNT RESERVATIONS

To save money, **look into discount reservations services** with toll-free numbers, which use their buying power to get a better price on hotels, airline tickets, even car rentals. When booking a room, always **call the hotel's local toll-free number** (if one is available) rather than the central reservations number—you'll often get a better price. Always ask about special packages or corporate rates.

When shopping for the best deal on hotels and car rentals, **look for guaranteed exchange rates,** which protect you against a falling dollar. With your rate locked in, you won't pay more, even if the price goes up in the local currency. Many large agencies in the United States offer special prices if you prepay for a rental car in U.S. dollars.

Electricity

To use your U.S.-purchased electric-powered equipment, **bring a converter and adapter.** The electrical current in Turkey is 220 volts, 50 cycles alternating current (AC); wall outlets take Continental-type plugs, with two or three round prongs.

Don't use 110-volt outlets marked FOR SHAVERS ONLY for high-wattage appliances such as blow-dryers. Most laptops operate equally well on 110 and 220 volts and so require only an adapter.

Embassies/Consulates

If your passport is lost or stolen, contact your consulate immediately.

➤ CONTACT INFORMATION: **Australian Consulate** (58 Tepecik Yolu, Etiler, tel. 212/257–7050). **Canadian Consulate** (107/3 Büyükdere Cad., Gayrettepe, tel. 212/272–5174). **U.K. Consulate** (34 Meşrutiyet Cad., Tepebaşı, tel. 212/293–7540). **U.S. Consulate** (104 Meşrutiyet Cad., Tepebaşı, tel. 212/251–3602).

Emergencies

Ask a Turk to call an emergency number for you because it's unlikely that an English-speaking person will answer, even at the Tourism Police. Bystanders will usually try their utmost to help. The Turkish words for ambulance, doctor, and police—*ambulans, doktor,* and *polis,* respectively—all sound about the same as their English equivalents, as does *telefon* for telephone.

There's a pharmacy in every neighborhood, and all post the name and address of the nearest one open around the clock.

The names of 24-hour pharmacies are also available through the directory inquiries service, although it is advisable to ask a Turkish speaker to make the call. Taksim, one good pharmacy, is centrally located in the Taksim district.

➤ CONTACTS: **Ambulance** (tel. 112). **Emergency (police, etc.)** (tel. 155). **International Hospital Ambulance** (tel. 212/663–3000). **Tourism Police** (tel. 212/527–4503).

➤ HOSPITALS: **American Hospital** (Güzelbahçe Sok. 20, Nişantaşı, tel. 212/231–4050). **German Hospital** (Siraselviler Cad. 119, Taksim, tel. 212/293–2150). **International Hospital** (Istanbul Cad. 82, Yeşilköy, tel. 212/663–3000).

➤ PHARMACIES: **Directory Inquiries Service** (tel. 118). **Taksim** (İstiklal Cad. 17, tel. 212/244–3195). **24-hour pharmacies hotline** (tel. 111).

Etiquette & Behavior

Turks set great store in politeness. Although Turks are a very tactile people, **be very careful about initiating physical contact,** as misunderstandings are easy. Overt public physical displays of affection between the sexes are still not widespread.

Turks shake hands as a greeting, although this is more common between men than between women. For handshakes between the sexes, unless the Turkish woman is obviously highly Westernized, a foreign male should leave it up to her. It is also usually best for foreign women to allow a Turkish man to initiate the handshake. Occasionally, very religious Turkish males will pointedly avoid shaking a woman's hand. It is common for friends of the same sex to greet each other by kissing on both cheeks using a stylized, cheek-to-cheek "air-kiss." However, it is unusual for two people of the opposite sex to kiss cheeks at all, and you should **be wary of kissing someone of the opposite sex in any manner** unless you are confident it will not be misinterpreted.

If you visit Turks in their homes, **take off your shoes on entering.** You're not expected to bring gifts, but a small token is always appreciated. Chances are the lady of the house will have gone to considerable trouble to prepare so you should **go with an empty stomach and at least try the dishes that are offered to you.** In appreciation, it is traditional to say *ellerinize sağlık* (ell-lair-in-izeh sah-luk), which translates literally as, "May your hands be healthy." No offense will be taken if you don't manage to say it, but it will be much appreciated if you do.

BUSINESS ETIQUETTE

Business negotiations are usually conducted in a relaxed atmosphere, and the business of the day may be padded with polite conversation and the ubiquitous cups of tea. It's usually a good idea not to force the pace. Punctuality is appreciated, but chronic traffic congestion means most businesspeople are used to people arriving a little late for appointments. A telephone call to **warn of a late arrival** is appreciated.

MOSQUES

Turkey is comparatively lenient regarding the visiting of mosques—in many Muslim countries, non-Muslims are strictly forbidden to enter them at all. Most mosques in Turkey are open to the public during the day. Prayer sessions, called *namaz,* last from 30 to 40 minutes and are observed five times daily. These times are based on the position of the sun, so they vary throughout the seasons but are generally around sunrise (between 5 and 7), at lunchtime (around noon or 1, when the sun is directly overhead), in the afternoon (around 3 or 4), at sunset (usually between 5 and 7), and at bedtime (at 9 or 10)—a daily list of prayer times can be found in Turkish newspapers. During namaz it's best not to enter a mosque. Non-Muslims should especially **avoid visiting mosques midday on Friday,** when Muslims are required to congregate and worship.

Women must **cover their arms and legs** inside a mosque. Men should **avoid wearing shorts** as well. Women should not enter a mosque without first covering their heads with a scarf, though some guardians will overlook it when a female tourist does not cover her head.

Before entering a mosque, **remove your shoes.** There is usually an attendant, and shoes are generally safe. If you feel uncomfortable about leaving them, you can always carry them in your backpack or handbag. It is considered offensive for a non-Muslim to sit down in a mosque (many tourists do sit down despite the signs requesting them not to). It is also advisable to show respect for both the sanctity of the mosque and the piety of those who might be praying in it by talking only in whispers. On no account should you try to take photographs inside the mosque, particularly of people praying.

A small donation is usually requested for the upkeep of the mosque. The equivalent of approximately 50¢ to US$1 is appropriate. Some mosques heavily visited by tourists may also have a "shoe keeper," who will ask for a tip.

Gay & Lesbian Travel

Openly gay men and women are still not generally accepted in Turkey, and the recent revival in conservative Islamic sentiment has made matters more difficult. Lesbians are virtually invisible in Turkey. Gay men are more visible (a few well-known singers are generally acknowledged to be gay), and there are gay bars in the major cities. There have been attempts to start a gay movement and to organize conferences on gay rights and other such events, but these have invariably been broken up by the police. Overt displays of affection between gay foreigners will undoubtedly attract stares at the very least.

Health

No serious health risks are associated with travel to Turkey. No vaccinations are required for entry. However, to avoid problems at customs, diabetics carrying needles and syringes should

carry a letter from their physician confirming their need for insulin injections. Rabies can be a problem in Turkey, occasionally even in Istanbul. If bitten or scratched by a dog or cat about which you have suspicions, go to the nearest pharmacy and ask for assistance.

FOOD & DRINK

Tap water is heavily chlorinated and supposedly safe to drink in cities and resorts. It's best to play it safe, however, and stick to *şişe suyu* (bottled still water), *maden suyu* (bottled sparkling mineral water), or *maden sodası* (carbonated mineral water), which are better tasting and inexpensive. Otherwise, Turkish food is relatively safe.

OVER-THE-COUNTER REMEDIES

Many over-the-counter remedies available in Western countries can also be found in Turkish pharmacies, which are usually well stocked. Even a Turkish pharmacist who doesn't speak English will often be able to recognize a specific remedy, particularly if you write the name down, and find an appropriate alternative if that medication is not available.

Holidays

January 1 (New Year's Day); March 5–8 (Kurban Bayramı, an important religious holiday, honoring Abraham's willingness to sacrifice his son to God); April 23 (National Independence Day); May 19 (Atatürk's Commemoration Day, celebrating his birthday and the day he landed in Samsun, starting the independence movement); August 30 (Zafer Bayramı, or Victory Day, commemorating Turkish victories over Greek forces in 1922, during Turkey's War of Independence); October 29 (Cumhuriyet Bayramı, or Republic Day, celebrating Atatürk's proclamation of the Turkish republic in 1923); November 10 (the anniversary of Atatürk's death, commemorated most notably by a nationwide moment of silence at 9:05 AM); December 16–18 (Şeker Bayramı, marking the end of Ramadan).

Please bear in mind that Muslim religious holidays are based on the lunar calendar and shift back about 10 days each year. The dates given here for the Şeker and Kurban holidays are for 2001. In 2002 the dates for the Kurban Bayramı and Şeker Bayramı will be February 22–25 and December 5–7, respectively.

Many businesses and government offices close at midday, usually either 12:30 or 1, on the day before major holidays such as the religious bayrams and Republic Day. If a religious holiday takes up three or four days of a working week, the government will often declare the rest of the week an official holiday as well. However, such decisions are usually made less than a month before the holiday actually begins. For example, in 2001, the government will probably make Friday, March 9, an official holiday, effectively extending the Kurban Bayramı from Saturday March 3 to Sunday March 11.

Language

In 1928 Atatürk launched sweeping language reforms that, over a period of six weeks, replaced Arabic script with the Latin-based alphabet and eliminated many Arabic and Persian words from the Turkish language.

English, German, and sometimes French are widely spoken in hotels, restaurants, and shops. **Try learning a few basic Turkish words**; it will be appreciated.

Lodging

Confirm reservations more than once, particularly at hotels in popular destinations. Phone reservations are not always honored, so it's a good idea to fax the hotel and **get a written confirmation** of your reservations, as well as to call again before you arrive. If you want air-conditioning, make sure to ask about it when you reserve.

Asking to see the room in advance is accepted practice. It will probably be much more basic than the well-decorated reception

area. Check for noise, especially if the room faces a street or is anywhere near a nightclub or disco, and **look for window screens and mosquito coils**—small, flat disks that, when lighted, emit an unscented vapor that keeps biting insects away.

Assume that hotels operate on the **European Plan** (EP, with no meals) unless we specify they use either the **Continental Plan** (CP, with a Continental breakfast), **Breakfast Plan** (BP, with a full breakfast) or the **Modified American Plan** (MAP, with breakfast and dinner) or are **all-inclusive** (including all meals and most activities).

HOSTELS

No matter what your age, you can **save on lodging costs by staying at hostels.** Hostels run about $10–$25 per night. There are two youth hostels in Istanbul and many student residences also serve as such. Otherwise, you can usually find inexpensive lodging in *pansiyons* (☞ *below*).

HOTELS

The standard Turkish hotel room, which you will encounter endlessly throughout the country, is clean, with bare walls, low wood-frame beds (usually a single bed, twin beds, or, less often, a double), and industrial carpeting or kilims on the floor. However, less expensive properties will probably have plumbing and furnishings that leave much to be desired. If you want a double bed, go to a more expensive property, either Turkish or Western style. All hotels listed have private bath unless otherwise noted.

PANSIYONS

These small, family-run places are a common option. They range from charming old homes decorated in antiques to tiny, utilitarian rooms done in basic modern. As a rule, they are inexpensive and scrupulously clean. Private baths are common, though they are rudimentary—stall showers, toilets with sensitive plumbing. A simple breakfast is typically included.

Mail & Shipping

Post offices are painted bright yellow and have PTT (Post, Telegraph, and Telephone) signs on the front. The central post offices are open Monday through Saturday from 8 AM to 9 PM, Sunday from 9 to 7. Smaller ones are open Monday through Saturday between 8:30 and 5.

POSTAL RATES

Rates are frequently adjusted to keep pace with inflation, but the cost of sending a letter or postcard remains nominal. Shipping a 10-pound rug home via surface mail will cost about $25 and take from two to six months.

RECEIVING MAIL

If you're uncertain where you'll be staying, have mail sent to Poste Restante, Merkez Posthanesi (Central Post Office).

SHIPPING PARCELS

It is usually quicker and safer to carry your purchases with you, even if you have to pay excess baggage, to avoid having them become damaged or lost in transit. Other alternatives, such as courier services or shipping companies, are quicker and more reliable but often very expensive.

Money Matters

Turkey is the least expensive of the Mediterranean countries. Although inflation hovers between 70% and 100%, frequent devaluations of the Turkish lira keep prices fairly stable against foreign currencies (which is why prices in this guide are listed in U.S. dollars). Only in Istanbul do costs approach those in Europe, and then only at top establishments.

ATMS

ATMs can be found throughout the city. Many accept international credit cards or bank cards (a strip of logos is usually displayed above the ATM). Almost all ATMs have a language key that enables you to read the instructions in

English. To use your card in Turkey, your PIN must be four digits long.

Using an ATM is one of the easiest ways to get money in Turkey. Generally the exchange rate is based on the Turkish Central Bank or the exchange rate according to your bank. The exchange rate is almost always better through an ATM than with traveler's checks, but not as good as when exchanging cash.

CREDIT CARDS

Credit cards are accepted throughout the city (primarily Visa and MasterCard, and sometimes American Express or Diner's Club). Note, however, that many budget-oriented restaurants or hotels do not accept credit cards.

If you're planning to get a cash advance on your credit card while in Turkey, it's a good idea to **inform the credit company,** as companies have been known to put freezes on credit cards because they assumed the transactions in Turkey were fraudulent.

Throughout this guide, the following abbreviations are used: **AE,** American Express; **DC,** Diner's Club; **MC,** Master Card; and **V,** Visa.

CURRENCY

The monetary unit is the Turkish lira (TL), which comes in bank notes of 100,000; 500,000; 1,000,000; 5,000,000; and 10,000,000. Smaller denominations come in coins of 10,000; 25,000; 50,000; and 100,000. In fall 2000 the exchange rate was TL 687,800 to the U.S. dollar, TL 449,752 to the Canadian dollar, and TL 983,554 to the pound sterling.

Note that Turks often quote prices minus the last three zeros, or even the last five or six zeros. For 250,000,000 TL, for instance, a shopkeeper will say *ici bucuk* (two and a half) or will mark the price tag 250 TL.

In early 2000 the Turkish Central Bank announced plans to shave six zeros off the value of the Turkish lira and introduce a new Turkish lira worth around $2, probably in January 2002.

CURRENCY EXCHANGE

Because Turkey constantly devalues its currency, wait to change money until you arrive. To avoid lines at airport exchange booths, however, **get a bit of local currency before you leave home.**

A growing number of privately operated exchange booths offer significantly better rates than hotels or banks. Paying in American dollars, too, can sometimes lead to an extra discount on your purchase.

Although fees charged for ATM transactions may be higher abroad than at home, Cirrus and Plus exchange rates are excellent because they are based on wholesale rates offered only by major banks. You won't do as well at exchange booths in airports or rail and bus stations, in hotels, in restaurants, or in stores, although you may find their hours more convenient.

➤ **Exchange Services: International Currency Express** (tel. 888/278–6628 for orders, www.foreignmoney.com). **Thomas Cook Currency Services** (tel. 800/287–7362 for telephone orders and retail locations, www.us.thomascook.com).

TRAVELER'S CHECKS

Many places in Turkey, even in Istanbul, do not take traveler's checks. And even those that do invariably offer better exchange rates for cash. Lost or stolen checks, however, can usually be replaced within 24 hours, so you may want the added security of traveler's checks even if they prove a little more expensive. To ensure a speedy refund, **buy your own traveler's checks—don't let someone else pay for them**: irregularities like this can cause delays. The person who bought the checks should make the call to request a refund.

Packing

Turkey is an informal country, so leave the fancy clothes at home. Men will find a jacket and tie appropriate only for top

restaurants. For more modest establishments a blazer will more than suffice. Women should avoid overly revealing outfits and short skirts. Shorts are acceptable for hiking through ruins but not for touring mosques. The importance of a sturdy, comfortable pair of shoes cannot be exaggerated.

Light cottons are best for summer. Sunscreen and sunglasses will come in handy. It's a good idea to **carry some toilet paper with you at all times.** You'll need mosquito repellent for eating outside from March through October, and soap if you're staying in more moderately priced hotels.

Passports & Visas

When traveling internationally, **carry your passport** even if you don't need one (it's always the best form of I.D.) and **make two photocopies of the data page** (one for someone at home and another for you, carried separately from your passport). If you lose your passport, promptly call the nearest embassy or consulate and the local police.

ENTERING TURKEY

Citizens of Australia, Canada, and New Zealand need only a valid passport to enter Turkey for stays of up to 90 days. U.K. citizens need a valid passport and a visa for stays of up to 90 days. Visas can be issued at the Turkish embassy or consulate before you go, or at the point of entry; the cost is £10.

All U.S. citizens, even infants, need a valid passport and a visa to enter Turkey for stays of up to 90 days. Visas can be issued at the Turkish embassy or consulate before you go, or at the point of entry; the cost is $45 and must be paid in American dollars.

Even though visas are multiple entry and usually valid for 90 days, they cannot be issued for periods longer than the validity of the passport you present. If your passport has less than a month to run, you may not be given a visa at all. Check the validity of your passport before applying for the visa. Turkish officials may impose stiff fines for an overstay on your visa.

PASSPORT OFFICES

➤ **Australian Citizens: Australian Passport Office** (tel. 131–232, www.dfat.gov.au/passports).

➤ **Canadian Citizens: Passport Office** (tel. 819/994–3500 or 800/567–6868, www.dfait-maeci.gc.ca/passport).

➤ **New Zealand Citizens: New Zealand Passport Office** (tel. 04/494–0700, www.passports.govt.nz).

➤ **U.K. Citizens: London Passport Office** (tel. 0990/210–410) for fees and documentation requirements and to request an emergency passport.

➤ **U.S. Citizens: National Passport Information Center** (tel. 900/225–5674; calls are 35¢ per min for automated service, $1.05 per min for operator service).

Rest Rooms

Public facilities are common in the tourist areas and at archeological sites and other attractions; in most, a custodian will ask you to pay a small fee (100 TL or so). In virtually all public facilities, including those in all but the fanciest restaurants, toilets are Turkish style (squatters) and toilet paper is often not provided (to cleanse themselves, Turks use a pitcher of water set next to the toilet). Sometimes it is possible to purchase toilet paper from the custodian, but you are well advised to carry a supply with you as part of your travel gear. Alas, standards of rest room cleanliness tend to be a bit low compared to those in Western Europe and America.

Safety

Violent crime against strangers is still very rare in Turkey. Istanbul is considerably safer than its Western counterparts. You should nevertheless **watch your valuables,** as pickpockets, although not as common as in the United States or Europe, do operate in the major cities and tourist areas.

WOMEN IN TURKEY

Although Turkey is a generally safe destination for women traveling alone, in heavily touristed areas, women unaccompanied by men are likely to be approached and sometimes followed.

Some Turkish men are genuinely curious about women from other lands and really do want only to "practice their English." Still, be forewarned that the willingness to converse can easily be misconstrued as something more meaningful.

As for clothing, Turkey is not the place for clothing that is short, tight, or bare, particularly away from the main tourist areas. Longer skirts and shirts and blouses with sleeves are what it takes here to look respectable. Though it may feel odd, covering your head with a scarf will make things easier on you (it's a good idea to have a scarf in your bag at all times). It also helps if you **have the manager of the hotel where you are staying call ahead** to the manager of your next hotel to announce your arrival—your next host will feel some responsibility to keep you out of harm's way.

As in any other country in the world, the best courses of action are simply to walk on if approached and to avoid potentially troublesome situations, such as deserted neighborhoods at night. Note that in Turkey many hotels, restaurants, and other eating spots identify themselves as being for an *aile* (family) clientele, and many restaurants have special sections for women and children. How comfortable you are with being alone will affect whether you like these areas, which are away from the action—and you may prefer to take your chances in the main room (though some establishments will resist seating you there).

When traveling alone by bus, you should **request a seat next to another woman.**

Taxes

The value-added tax, in Turkey called Katma Değer Vergisi, or KDV, is 17% on most goods and services. Hotels typically combine it with a service charge of 10% to 15%, and restaurants usually add a 15% service charge.

Value-added tax is nearly always included in quoted prices. Certain shops are authorized to refund the tax (you must ask). Within a month of leaving Turkey, mail the stamped invoice back to the shop, and a check will be mailed to you—in theory if not always in practice.

Taxis or Dolmuşes

Taxis are metered and inexpensive, costing about $1 for 1 km, or about ½ mi. Make sure the meter says *gündüz* (day rate); otherwise, you'll be overcharged as fares are 50% more expensive between midnight and 6 AM. **Don't ride in a taxi in which the meter doesn't work.** Avoid taxi drivers who choose roundabout routes, which cost more money, by having your hotel's attendant or a Turkish speaker talk to the driver before you get in. Note that saying the word *direkt* after giving your destination helps prevent you from getting an unplanned grand tour of town.

Most drivers do not speak English and may not know every street, so write down the name of the one you want and those nearby and the name of the neighborhood you're visiting. The vast majority of Istanbul taxi drivers are scrupulously honest—but in one commonly reported scam a driver will tell a foreigner customer unfamiliar with the local currency that he or she has handed over the wrong amount of Turkish lira, so be mindful when paying. It is inadvisable to agree on a fare with a driver unless you know for certain it is cheaper than the metered fare. Tipping is not required, though many taxi drivers expect tourists to round up the price of the ride to the nearest hundred thousand lira.

Dolmuşes (shared taxis), many of which are bright yellow minibuses, run along various routes. You can sometimes hail a dolmuş on the street, and as with taxis, dolmuş stands are marked by signs. The destination is shown on either a roof sign or a card in the front window. Dolmuş stands are placed at regular intervals, and the vehicles wait for customers to climb in. Though the savings over a private taxi are significant, you may find the quarters a little too close for comfort, particularly in summer.

Telephones

Telephone numbers in Turkey have seven-digit local numbers preceded by a three-digit city code. Intercity lines are reached by dialing 0 before the area code and number. In Istanbul, European and Asian Istanbul have separate area codes: The code for much of European Istanbul is 212 (making the number look like it's in New York City—but it's not), and the code for Asian Istanbul (numbers beginning with 3 or 4) is 216.

AREA & COUNTRY CODES

The country code for Turkey is 90. When dialing a Turkish number from abroad, drop the initial 0 from the local area code. The country code for the United States is 1, 61 for Australia, 1 for Canada, 64 for New Zealand, and 44 for the U.K.

DIRECTORY & OPERATOR ASSISTANCE

For international operator services, dial 115. Intercity telephone operators seldom speak English, although international operators usually have some basic English. If you need international dialing codes and assistance or phone books, you can also go to the nearest post office.

INTERNATIONAL CALLS

To make an international call from a public phone in Turkey, dial 00, then dial the country code, area or city code, and the number. Expect to pay about $3–$5 per minute.

LOCAL CALLS

Inside Istanbul you don't need to dial the code for other numbers with the same code, but you need to dial the code (0212 or 0216) when calling from the European to the Asian side of the city or vice versa. All local cellular calls are classed as long distance, and you need to dial the city code for every number.

LONG-DISTANCE CALLS

To call long-distance within Turkey, dial 131 if you need operator assistance; otherwise dial 0, then dial the city code and number.

PUBLIC PHONES

Most pay phones are blue push-button models, although a few older, operator-controlled telephones are still in use. Directions in English and other languages are often posted in phone booths.

Public phones either use phone cards or *jetons* (tokens). Tokens are available in 7¢ and 30¢ denominations, while phone cards come in denominations of 30 ($2), 60 ($3.50), and 100 ($5) units; buy a 60 or 100 for long-distance calls within Turkey, a 30 for local usage. Both tokens and phone cards can be purchased at post offices and, for a small markup, at some corner stores, newspaper vendors, and street stalls. However, they can sometimes be difficult to find, so it's a good idea to buy one at the first opportunity.

To make a local call, insert your phone card or deposit a 7¢ token, wait until the light at the top of the phone goes off, and then dial the number.

Time

Istanbul is 2 hours ahead of London, 7 hours ahead of New York, 10 hours ahead of Los Angeles and Vancouver, 11 hours behind Auckland and 9 hours behind Sydney and Melbourne.

Tipping

In restaurants a 10%–15% charge is added to the bill in all but inexpensive fast-food spots. However, since this money does not necessarily find its way to your waiter, leave an additional 10% on the table. In top establishments waiters expect tips of 10%–15% in addition to the service charge. Although it's acceptable to include the tip on your bill in restaurants that accept credit cards, a small tip in cash is much appreciated.

Hotel porters expect about $2. Taxi drivers are becoming used to foreigners giving them something; round off the fare to the nearest 100,000 TL. At Turkish baths staff members who attend to you expect to share a tip of 30%–35% of the bill. Don't worry about missing them—they'll be lined up expectantly on your departure.

Tour guides often expect a tip. Offer as much or (as little) as you feel the person deserves, usually $4–$5 per day if you were happy with the guide. If you've been with the guide for a number of days, tip more.

Tours & Packages

Because everything is prearranged on a prepackaged tour or independent vacation, you'll spend less time planning—and often get it all at a good price.

BOOKING WITH AN AGENT

Travel agents are excellent resources. But it's a good idea to collect brochures from several agencies as some agents' suggestions may be influenced by relationships with tour and package firms that reward them for volume sales. If you have a special interest, **find an agent with expertise in that area**; ASTA (☞ Travel Agencies, *below*) has a database of specialists worldwide.

Make sure your travel agent knows the accommodations and other services of the place they're recommending. Ask about the hotel's location, room size, beds, and whether it has a pool, room service, or programs for children, if you care about these. Has your agent been there in person or sent others whom you can contact?

Do some homework on your own, too: local tourism boards can provide information about lesser-known and small-niche operators, some of which may sell only direct.

BUYER BEWARE

Each year consumers are stranded or lose their money when tour operators—even large ones with excellent reputations—go out of business. So **check out the operator.** Ask several travel agents about its reputation, and try to **book with a company that has a consumer-protection program** (look for information in the company's brochure). In the United States members of the National Tour Association and the United States Tour Operators Association are required to set aside funds to cover your payments and travel arrangements in the event the company defaults. It's also a good idea to choose a company that participates in the American Society of Travel Agents' Tour Operator Program (TOP); ASTA will act as mediator in any disputes between you and your tour operator.

Remember that the more your package or tour includes, the better you can predict the ultimate cost of your vacation. Make sure you know exactly what is covered, and **beware of hidden costs.** Are taxes, tips, and transfers included? Entertainment and excursions? These can add up.

➤ TOUR-OPERATOR RECOMMENDATIONS: **American Society of Travel Agents** (☞ Travel Agencies, *below*). **National Tour Association** (NTA; 546 E. Main St., Lexington, KY 40508, tel. 606/226–4444 or 800/682–8886, www.ntaonline.com). **United States Tour Operators Association** (USTOA; 342 Madison Ave., Suite 1522, New York, NY 10173, tel. 212/599–6599 or 800/468–7862, fax 212/599–6744, www.ustoa.com).

Train Travel

The overnight sleeper from Istanbul to Ankara (*Ankara Ekspres*) is the most comfortable and convenient of the trains, with private compartments, attentive service, and a candlelighted dining car. There is also daytime service between Ankara and Istanbul and service between Istanbul and Edirne.

Fares are lower for trains than for buses (but trains are not as comfortable as buses), and round-trips cost less than two one-way tickets. Student discounts are 10% (30% from December through April). Ticket windows in railroad stations are marked GIŞELERI. Some post offices and authorized travel agencies also sell train tickets. It's advisable to **book in advance, in person, for seats on the best trains and for sleeping quarters.**

Trains from Europe and the west (and service is limited) arrive at Sirkeci Station, in Old Stamboul, near the Galata Bridge. Trains from Anatolia and the east come into Haydarpaşa Station, on the Asian side.

➤ INFORMATION: **Haydarpaşa Station** (tel. 216/336–0475). **Sirkeci Station** (tel. 212/527–0051).

PAYING

Most train stations do not accept credit cards or foreign exchange, so be prepared to pay in Turkish lira.

Travel Agencies

A good travel agent puts your needs first. Look for an agency that has been in business at least five years, emphasizes customer service, and has someone on staff who specializes in your destination. In addition, **make sure the agency belongs to a professional trade organization.** The American Society of Travel Agents (ASTA), with 27,000 agents in some 170 countries, is the largest and most influential in the field. Operating under the motto "Integrity in Travel," it maintains and enforces a strict code of ethics and will step in to help mediate any agent-client disputes if necessary. ASTA also maintains a Web site that includes a directory of agents. (If a travel agency is also acting as your tour operator, *see* Buyer Beware in Tours & Packages, *above*.)

➤ LOCAL AGENT REFERRALS: **American Society of Travel Agents** (ASTA; tel. 800/965–2782 24-hr hot line, fax 703/684–8319, www.astanet.com). **Association of British Travel Agents** (68–71 Newman St., London W1P 4AH, tel. 020/7637–2444, fax 020/7637–0713, www.abtanet.com). **Association of Canadian Travel Agents** (1729 Bank St., Suite 201, Ottawa, Ontario K1V 7Z5, tel. 613/237–3657, fax 613/521–0805). **Australian Federation of Travel Agents** (Level 3, 309 Pitt St., Sydney 2000, tel. 02/9264–3299, fax 02/9264–1085, www.afta.com.au). **Travel Agents' Association of New Zealand** (Box 1888, Wellington 10033, tel. 04/499–0104, fax 04/499–0827).

Visitor Information

➤ IN ISTANBUL: **Turkish Ministry of Tourism** (Atatürk Airport, tel. 212/663–0793; Istanbul Hilton, Cumhuriyet Cad., Harbiye, tel. 212/233–0592; International Maritime Passenger Terminal, Karaköy Meyd., tel. 212/249–5776; In Sultanahmet district, Divan Yolu Cad. 3, tel. 212/518–1802; and In Beyoğlu district, Meşrutiyet Cad. 57, tel. 212/243–3731).

➤ TURKISH TOURISM OFFICES ABROAD: Australia (280 George St., Suite 101, Sydney, NSW-2000, tel. 02/9223–3055). Canada (Constitution Sq., 360 Albert St., Suite 801, Ottawa, Ontario K1R 7X7,, tel. 613/230–8654, fax 613/230–3683). U.K. (170–173 Piccadilly, 1st floor, London W1V 9DD, tel. 020/7629–7771). U.S. (821 UN Plaza, New York, NY 10017, tel. 212/687–2194, fax 212/599–7568; 1717 Massachusetts Ave. NW, Suite 306, Washington, DC 20036, tel. 202/429–9844, fax 202/429–5649).

➤ U.S. GOVERNMENT ADVISORIES: **U.S. Department of State** (Overseas Citizens Services Office, Room 4811 N.S., 2201 C St. NW, Washington, DC 20520, tel. 202/647–5225 for interactive hot line, 301/946–4400 for computer bulletin board, fax 202/647–3000 for interactive hot line); enclose a self-addressed, stamped business-size envelope.

Web Sites

Do check out the World Wide Web when you're planning your trip. You'll find everything from current weather forecasts to virtual tours. Fodor's Web site, www.fodors.com, is a great place to start your online travels.

➤ **URLs: Republic of Turkey** (www.turkey.org). **Travel in Turkey** (www.mersina.com; www.turkiye-online.com; www.exploreturkey.com). **Turkish Tourist Office** (www.turizm.gov.tr/life.html).

When to Go

CLIMATE

Most tourists visit between April and the end of October. July and August are the busiest months (and the hottest). April through June and September and October offer more temperate weather, smaller crowds, and somewhat lower hotel prices. Istanbul tends to be hot in summer, cold in winter.

➤ Forecasts: **Weather Channel Connection** (tel. 900/932–8437), 95¢ per minute from a Touch-Tone phone.

CLIMATE IN ISTANBUL

Jan.	46F	8C	**May**	69F	21C	**Sept.**	76F	24C
	37	3		53	12		61	16
Feb.	47F	9C	**June**	77F	25C	**Oct.**	68F	20C
	36	2		60	16		55	13
Mar.	51F	11C	**July**	82F	28C	**Nov.**	59F	15C
	38	3		65	18		48	9
Apr.	60F	16C	**Aug.**	82F	28C	**Dec.**	51F	11C
	45	7		66	19		41	5

TURKISH VOCABULARY

Words and Phrases

ENGLISH	TURKISH	PRONUNCIATION
Basics		
Yes/no	Evet/hayır	*eh*-vet/*hi*-yer
Please	Lütfen	*lewt*-fen
Thank you	Teşekkür ederim	tay-shake-*kur* eh-day-*reem*
You're welcome	Rica ederim Bir şey değil	ree-*jah* eh-day-*reem* beer shay *day*-eel
Sorry	Özür dilerim	oh-*zewr* deel-air-eem
Sorry	Pardon	*pahr*-dohn
Good morning	Günaydın	goon-eye-*den*
Good day	Iyi günler	ee-yee gewn-*lair*
Good evening	Iyi akşamlar	ee-yee ank-shahm-*lahr*
Goodbye	Allahaısmarladık	*allah*-aw-ees-mar-law-deck
	Güle güle	*gew*-leh-gew-leh
Mr. (Sir)	Bey	by, bay
Mrs. Miss	Hanım	ha-nem
Pleased to meet you	Taniştiğimiza memnun oldum	tahnesh-tumu-*zah* *mam*-noon ohl-doom
How are you?	Nasılsınız?	*nah*-suhl-suh-nuhz

Numbers

one half	büçük	byoo-*chook*
one	bir	beer
two	iki	ee-*kee*
three	üc	ooch
four	dört	doort
five	beş	besh
six	altı	ahl-tuh
seven	yedi	yed-dee
eight	sekiz	sek-*keez*
nine	dokuz	doh-*kooz*
ten	on	ohn
eleven	onbir	*ohn*-beer
twelve	oniki	*ohn*-ee-kee
thirteen	onüç	*ohn-ooch*
fourteen	ondört	*ohn-doort*
fifteen	onbeş	*ohn*-besh
sixteen	onaltı	*ohn*-ahl-tuh
seventeen	onyedi	*ohn*-yed-dy
eighteen	onsekiz	*ohn*-sek-*keez*
nineteen	ondokuz	*ohn*-doh-*kooz*
twenty	yirmi	yeer-mee
twenty-one	yirmibir	*yeer*-mee-beer
thirty	otuz	oh-*tooz*
forty	kırk	kerk
fifty	elli	ehl-lee
sixty	altmış	*alt*-muhsh
seventy	yetmiş	*yeht*-meesh
eighty	seksen	sehk-san
ninety	doksan	dohk-*san*
one hundred	yüz	yewz
one thousand	bin	bean
one million	milyon	mill-ee-on

Days of the Week

Sunday	Pazar	pahz-*ahr*
Monday	Pazartesi	pahz-*ahr*-teh-see
Tuesday	Salı	sahl-luhl
Wednesday	Çarşamba	char-shahm-*bah*
Thursday	Perşembe	pair-shem-*beh*
Friday	Cuma	*joom*-ahz
Saturday	Cumartesi	joom-*ahr*-teh-see

Months

January	Ocak	oh-*jahk*
February	Şubat	shoo-*baht*
March	Mart	mart
April	Nisan	nee-*sahn*
May	Mayıs	my-us
June	Haziran	hah-zee-*rahn*
July	Temmuz	*tehm*-mooz
August	Ağustos	ah-oos-tohs
September	Eylül	ey-*lewl*
October	Ekim	eh-*keem*
November	Kasım	kah-suhm
December	Aralık	ah-rah-*luhk*

Useful Phrases

Do you speak English?	İngilizce biliyor musunuz?	in-*gee*-*leez*-jay bee-lee-*yohr*-moo-soo-nooz
I don't speak Turkish	Türkçe bilmiyorum	*tewrk*-cheh *beel*-mee-yohr-um
I don't understand	Anlamıyorum	ahn-*lah*-muh-yohr-um
I understand	Anlıyorum	ahn-*luh*-yohr-um
I don't know	Bilmiyorum	*beel*-meeh-yohr-um

I'm American/ I'm British	Amerikalıyım Ingilizim	ahm-ay-*ree*-kah-luh-yuhm *een*-gee-leez-eem
What's your name?	Isminiz nedir?	ees-mee-niz nay-deer
My name is . . .	Benim adım . . .	bay-*neem* ah-duhm
What time is it?	Saat kaç?	sah-aht *kahch*
How?	Nasıl?	*nah*-suhl
When?	Ne zaman?	*nay* zah-mahn
Yesterday	Dün	dewn
Today	Bugün	*boo*-goon
Tomorrow	Yarın	*yah*-ruhn
This morning/ afternoon	Bu sabah/ ögleden sonra	*boo* sah-bah/ *oi-lay*-den sohn-rah
Tonight	Bu gece	*boo* ge-jeh
What?	Efendim?/Ne?	*eh*-fan-deem/neh
What is it?	Nedir?	*neh*-deer
Why?	Neden/Niçin?	*neh*-den/*nee*-chin
Who?	Kim?	keem
Where is . . .	Nerede . . .	*nayr*-deh
. . . the train station?	. . . tren istasyonu?	tee-*rehn* ees-*tah*-syohn-oo
. . . the subway station?	. . . metro durağı?	metro doo-*raw*-uh
. . . the bus stop?	. . . otobüs durağı?	oh-toh-*bewse* dor-*ah*-uh
. . . the terminal? (airport)	. . . hava alanı?	hah-*vah* *ah*-lah-nuh

. . . the post office?	. . . postane?	post-*ahn*-eh
. . . the bank?	. . . banka?	*bahn*-kah
. . . the hotel?	. . . oteli?	oh-*tel-lee*
. . . the museum?	. . . müzesi?	mew-zay-*see*
. . . the hospital?	. . . hastane?	hahs-*tah*-neh
. . . the elevator?	. . . asansör?	ah-sahn-*sewr*
. . . the telephone?	. . . telefon?	teh-leh-*fohn*
Where are the restrooms?	Tuvalet nerede?	twah-*let* nayr-deh
Here/there	Burası/Orası	*boo*-rah-suh/ *ohr*-rah-suh
Left/right	sağ/sol	sah-ah/sohl
Is it near/ far?	Yakın mı?/ Uzak mı?	yah-*kuhn* muh/ ooz-*ahk*muh
I'd like . . .	. . . istiyorum	*ees*-tee-yohr-ruhm
. . . a room	. . . bir oda	beer oh-*dah*
. . . the key	. . . anahtarı	*ahn*-ah-tahr-uh
. . . a newspaper	. . . bir gazete	beer *gahz*-teh
. . . a stamp	. . . pul	pool
I'd like to buy . . .	. . . almak istiyorum	ahl-*mahk* ees-tee-your-ruhm
. . . cigarettes	. . . sigara	see-*gahr*-rah
. . . matches	. . . kibrit	*keeb*-reet
. . . city map	. . . şehir planı	shay-*heer plah*-nuh
. . . road map	. . . karayolları haritası	*kah*-rah-yoh-lahr-*uh* hah-ree-tah-*suh*
. . . magazine	. . . dergi	dair-gee
. . . envelopes	. . . zarf	zahrf

. . . writing paper	. . . mektup kağıdı	*make*-toop *kah*-uh-duh
. . . postcard	. . . kartpostal	cart-poh-stahl
How much is it?	Fiyatı ne kadar?	fee-yaht-uh *neh* kah-dahr
It's expensive/ cheap	pahalı/ucuz	pah-hah-*luh*/ oo-*jooz*
A little/a lot	Az/çok	ahz/choke
More/less	daha çok/daha az	da-ha choke/ da-ha ahz
Enough/too (much)	Yeter/çok fazla	*yay*-tehr/*choke* fahz-lah
I am ill/sick	Hastayım	*hahs*-tah-yum
Call a doctor	Doktor çağırın	dohk-toor *chah*-uh-run
Help!	Imdat!	eem-*daht*
Stop!	Durun!	doo-*roon*

Dining Out

A bottle of . . .	bir şişe . . .	*beer* shee-shay
A cup of . . .	bir fincan . . .	beer *feen*-jahn
A glass of . . .	bir bardak . . .	beer *bar*-dahk
Ashtray	kül tablası	kewl tah-blah-*suh*
Bill/check	hesap	heh-*sahp*
Bread	ekmek	ekmek
Breakfast	kahvaltı	*kah*-vahl-tuh
Butter	tereyağı	tay-*reh*-yah-uh
Cocktail/aperitif	kokteyl, içki	cocktail, *each*-key
Dinner	aksam yemeği	*ahk*-shahm yee-may-ee

Fixed-price menu	fiks menü	feex menu
Fork	çatal	*chah*-tahl
I am a vegetarian/ I don't eat meat	vejeteryenim/ et yemem	vegeterian-*eem*/ eht yeh-*mem*
I cannot eat . . .	. . . yiyemem	*yee*-yay-mem
I'd like to order . . .	. . . ısmarlamak isterim	us-mahr-lah-*mahk* ee-stair-eem
I'd like . . .	. . . isterim	ee-stair-*em*
I'm hungry/ thirsty	acıktım/ susadım	ah-*juck*-tum/ soo-sah-*dum*
Is service/the tip included?	servis fiyatı dahil mi?	sehr-rees *fee*-yah-tah dah-heel-*mee*
It's good/bad	güzel/güzel değil	gew-*zell*/gew-*zell* *day*-eel
It's hot/cold	sıcak/soğuk	suh-*jock*/soh-uk
Knife	bıçak	buh-*chahk*
Lunch	öğle yemeği	*oi*-leh *yeh*-may-ee
Menu	menü	meh-*noo*
Napkin	peçete	*peh*-cheh-teh
Pepper	karabiber	kah-*rah*-bee-behr
Plate	tabak	tah-*bahk*
Please give me . . .	lutfen bana . . . verirmisiniz	*loot*-fan bah-nah vair-*eer*-mee-see-niz
Salt	tuz	tooz
Spoon	kaşık	kah-*shuhk*

INDEX

FODOR'S POCKET ISTANBUL

EDITORS: Carissa Bluestone, Stephen Brewer

Editorial Contributors: Linda Cabasin, Gareth Jenkins

Editorial Production: Kristin Milavec

Maps: David Lindroth, *cartographer;* Bob Blake and Rebecca Baer, *map editors*

Design: Fabrizio La Rocca, *creative director;* Tigist Getachew, *art director;* Melanie Marin, *photo editor*

Production/Manufacturing: Colleen Ziemba

Cover Photograph: Robert Frerck/ Stone

COPYRIGHT

Second Edition

ISBN 0-679-00773-3

ISSN 1525-4402

IMPORTANT TIP

Although all prices, opening times, and other details in this book are based on information supplied to us at press time, changes occur all the time in the travel world, and Fodor's cannot accept responsibility for facts that become outdated or for inadvertent errors or omissions. So **always confirm information when it matters,** especially if you're making a detour to visit a specific place.

SPECIAL SALES

Fodor's Travel Publications are available at special discounts for bulk purchases for sales promotions or premiums. Special editions, including personalized covers, excerpts of existing guides, and corporate imprints, can be created in large quantities for special needs. For more information, contact your local bookseller or write to Special Markets, Fodor's Travel Publications, 280 Park Avenue, New York, NY 10017. Inquiries from Canada should be directed to your local Canadian bookseller or sent to Random House of Canada, Ltd., Marketing Department, 2775 Matheson Boulevard East, Mississauga, Ontario L4W 4P7. Inquiries from the United Kingdom should be sent to Fodor's Travel Publications, 20 Vauxhall Bridge Road, London SW1V 2SA, England.

PRINTED IN THE UNITED STATES OF AMERICA

10 9 8 7 6 5 4 3 2 1